A Handbook of Operating Systems

Dr.M. Sharada Varlakshmi

Priyanka Chaumwal

K. Shravani

M. Kamala

Published by

BONFRING®
Intellectual Integrity

AF528402

A Handbook of Operating Systems

Copyright © 2018 by Bonfring

All rights reserved. Authorized reprint of the edition published by Bonfring. No part of this book may be reproduced in any form without the written permission of the publisher.

Limits of Liability/Disclaimer of Warranty: The authors are solely responsible for the contents of the paper in this volume. The publishers or editors do not take any responsibility for the same in any manner. Errors, if any, are purely unintentional and readers are required to communicate such errors to the editors or publishers to avoid discrepancies in future. No warranty may be created or extended by sales or promotional materials. The advice and strategies contained herein may not be suitable for every situation. This work is sold with the understanding that the publisher is not engaged in rendering legal, accounting, or other professional services. If professional assistance is required, the services of a competent professional person should be sought. Further, reader should be aware that internet website listed in this work may have changed or disappeared between when this was written and when it is read.

Bonfring also publishes its books in a variety of electronic formats. Some content that appears in print may not be available in electronic books.

9 789387 862418 >

ISBN 978-93-87862-41-8

Authors

Dr.M. Sharada Varlakshmi

Priyanka Chaumwal

K. Shravani

M. Kamala

Bonfring

309, 2nd Floor,

5th Street Extension, Gandhipuram,

Coimbatore-641 012.

Tamilnadu, India.

E-mail: info@bonfring.org

Website: www.bonfring.org

Phone: 0422 4213231

Preface

Operating Systems are essential for any computers. So also, study on Operating Systems is a basic essentiality for any Computer Science Engineering course. This field is experiencing fast change, as computers are currently pervasive in practically every field of everyday life—from implanted gadgets in cars through the most refined arranging instruments for governments and worldwide firms. However the principle ideas remain genuinely clear, and it is on these that we base this book.

We composed this book as content for a starting course in Operating Systems at undergraduate level or at graduate level. We trust that students will likewise think that it's valuable. It gives an unmistakable depiction of the concepts that underlie Operating Systems. As prerequisites, we assume that the reader is familiar with basic data structures, computer organization, and a high-level language, such as C or Java.

Dr.M. Sharada Varlakshmi

Priyanka Chaumwal

K. Shravani

M. Kamala

Acknowledgement

This work would not have been possible without the support of our Secretary Shri. T.V Reddy and our Principal Dr.M. Narendra Kumar. We are especially indebted to all our colleagues, who have been supportive of our career goals and whc worked actively to provide us with the protected academic time to pursue those goals. We are grateful to all of those with whom we worked during this time of authoring the book. Our sincere thanks to all our family members for helping us and motivating us to publish this book **"A Handbook of Operating Systems"**.

Dr.M. Sharada Varlakshmi

Priyanka Chaumwal

K. Shravani

M. Kamala

Authors Profile

Dr.M. Sharada Varlakshmi is currently working as the HOD in the Department of Computer Science and Engineering at St. Peter's Engineering College, Hyderabad, Telangana, India. She has completed her PhD in Computer Science engineering from Jawaharlal Nehru Technology University, Hyderabad. She has ~18 years of teaching experience during which she has handled several subjects including Mobile Computing, DWDM, Linux Programming, Compiler Design, OOAD, Computer Networks, DBMS, CDS, PPL, and Operating Systems. In addition to this, she has also published more than 20 research papers in multiple international and national journals. She was also awarded the best faculty for the academic year 2017 – 2018 in St.Peter's Engineering College, Hyderabad.

Priyanka Chaumwal is currently working as an Assistant Professor in the Department of Computer Science and Engineering at St. Peter's Engineering College, Hyderabad, Telangana, India. She has done her M.Tech from Jodhpur National University and her B.Tech from Amaravati University in Computer Science and Engineering. She has published five research papers in International Journals and was awarded the first place for National level Poster presentation. She was also awarded the best faculty for the academic year 2018 – 2019 in St.Peter's Engineering College, Hyderabad.

K. Shravani is currently working as a Assistant Professor in the Department of Computer Science and Engineering at St. Peter's Engineering College, Hyderabad, Telangana, India. She has done her M.Tech from Jawaharlal Nehru Technological University and her B.Tech from Jawarharlal Technological University Hyderabad in CSE. She has published 6 research papers in International Journals and She has attended 5 FDPs.

M. Kamala is currently working as an Assistant Professor in the Department of Computer Science and Engineering at St. Peter's Engineering College, Hyderabad, Telangana, India. M.Tech in Computer Science and Engineering at Jawaharlal Nehru Technological university, Hyderabad. She has Published 10 research papers in various National and International Journals and International Conference. She was awarded the best faculty for the academic year 2017 – 2018 in St.Peter's Engineering College, Hyderabad, Telangana, India. She is a member in ISTE. Her Research area includes Cloud Computing.

CHAPTERS	CONTENTS	PAGE NO

CHAPTER 1

INTRODUCTION TO OPERATING SYSTEMS

1.1. Objectives

In this unit, you will be able to learn about:

- Basic Organization of Computer Systems.
- Operating system, functions, history and Evolution.
- Assembler, linker, loader, compiler.
- The services that an Operating System provides to the processes, other applications, and the users.
- Operating system services and its various components.
- Time-sharing, Buffering and Spooling.
- Multi-programming and Multi-tasking.

1.2. Introduction

An operating system acts as an interface between the user of a computer or a machine and the machine's hardware. The main purpose of operating system is to provide a user-friendly environment where a user can be able to perform his operations and execute programs in a convenient and efficient manner.

An operating system is a combination of System software and hardware that manages the operations of software and hardware simultaneously. The hardware must provide the most appropriate methods to ensure the exact operation of computer system and to prevent user programs from interrupting the usual functional behaviour of the system.

An Operating system is a software that provides the environment where the user can execute various programs. Internally, the OS vary mostly in their interface and the workplace since they are being organized along several different lines. The design of a new OS is a major task. It is most important that the aim and application of system will be well defined before designing begins.

We can view the task of an Operating system from various vantage points. One of the views focus on the system provides, and the other focuses on the interface that the OS makes it available for the programmers and users; and the third one focusses on the components of an OS and their interconnections.

1.3. Operating System

1.3.1. Definition of Operating System

- An operating system is a program which controls and maintains the execution of any application and acts as intermediary interface between the user and the machine hardware.
- The most common definition is that the Operating-System is referred to as the program which is always under the execution state (generally known as the kernel).
- Operating system is the software that is concerned with the resource allocation and services such as processors, memory, information and devices. The Operating system contains the programs to manage those resources such as Scheduler, memory management module, traffic controller, I/O programs, and a file system.

1.3.2. Functions of Operating System

An Operating system should perform the following functions:

- **Efficiency:** It should allow the computer resources to be used in conveniently and efficiently.
- **Convenience:** It should make a computer more convenient to use.
- **Ability to Evolve:** An OS must be constructed in a manner to be reprogrammed as per the requirement.

1.3.3. Operating System as User Interface

- Every general-purpose computer consists of the hardware, Operating system applications and application programs. The hardware consists of memory, CPU, ALU, I/O Devices, Peripheral device and storage device. System program comprises of compilers, loaders, OS, editors, etc. the application program is comprised of business program and database program.
- The conceptual view of a Computer system is shown in the fig. 1.1.
- Every Computer must have an OS to run other applications. The OS coordinates the use of hardware of the system among the various system programs and application programs.
- The Operating system is a combination of special programs or processes that allows it to work efficiently. It performs basic tasks such as recognizing input from the keyboard, keeping track of files and directories on that particular memory disk, while sending the output to the monitor and maintaining the peripheral devices.

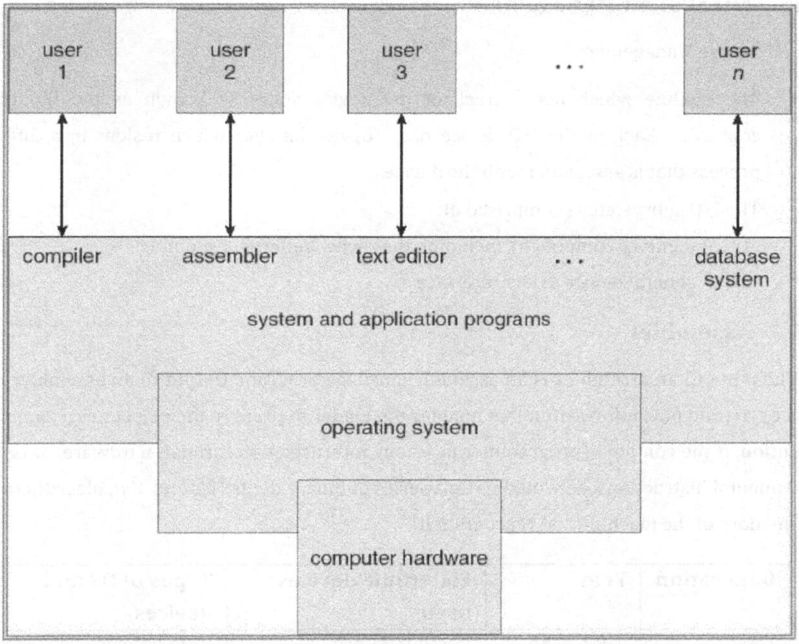

Conceptual View of a Computer System

- Operating system is designed to serve two basic purposes:
    1. It controls the memory allocation and the resource allocation among the various tasks and users of a Computer system.
    2. It provides an interface between the computer hardware and programmer that simplifies and makes feasible for coding, creation, debugging of application programs.
- The OS must support the following operations:
    1. It should provide the facilities to create, modify and reuse the processes and programs and data files using an editor.
    2. It should provide the access to the compiler to translate the program to the machine understandable language.
    3. It should provide a loader program to move the Source code (Compiled program code) to the Computer memory for execution of the program.
    4. It has to provide the routines that can handle the details of the I/O programmer.

1.4. I/O System Management

I/O System Management.

- The module which keeps track of the device status is known as the I/O traffic controller. Each of the I/O device has a device handler which resides in a different process that is associated with the device.
- The I/O subsystem is comprised of:
  1. A memory component, including the cache, buffer and spooling.
  2. A general device driver interface.

1.5. Assembler

The input to an assembler is an assembly language program. Output to an assembler is an object program plus information that enables the loader to prepare the object program for the execution. If the computer programmer faces any interpretetion through hardware, or certain fundamental instructions, he would write a series of binary digits (0's and 1's), place them into the memory of the machine and reprogram it.

Generation	Year	Electronic devices used	Types of OS and devices
First	1945 – 55	Vacuum tubes	Plug boards
Second	1955 – 1965	Transistors	Batch system
Third	1965 – 1980	Integrated Circuit (IC)	Multiprogramming
Fourth	Since 1980	Large scale integration	PC

1.6. Compiler

The high-level languages for example – COBOL, FORTRAN, PL/I and ALGOL, are processed by the compilers and the interpreters. Compiler is a program or combination of processes which can accept a source program in a user-friendly language and produces a corresponding Source code or object program. An Interpreter is a program that seems to execute a source code as a machine language.

1.7. Loader

A loader is a kind of routine that loads an object program and gets it ready for execution. There are various loading schemes like absolute, relocating and direct linking. The loader generally loads, relocates and links the object program. Loader is a program that relocates the programs into the memory and prepares them for execution.

1.8. History of Operating System

Operating systems have undergone a major evolution in the past few years. The history of the Operating system is shown in the table below.

1.9. Operating System Services

- An operating system provides services to programs and to those users individually for each program. The services provided by each operating system is different for each application.
- Operating system makes the programmer to complete the tasks easier.
- The Operating system provides the following services as listed below.
  1. Program Execution
  2. File system Manipulation
  3. Communications
  4. I/O Operations
  5. Error detection

1. ***Program execution:*** Operating system loads a program into memory and executes the program. The program must be able to end its execution, either normally or abnormally.
2. ***File system manipulation*** : Program needs to read a file or write a file. The operating system gives the permission to the program for operation on file.
3. ***Communication :*** Data transfer between two processes is required for some time. The both processes are on the one computer or on different computer but connected through computer network. Communication may be implemented by two methods:
   a. Shared memory.
   b. Message passing.
4. ***I/O Operation*** : I/O means any file or any specific I/O device. Program may require any I/O device while running. So operating system must provide the required I/O resources.
5. ***Error detection*** : Error may occur in CPU, in I/O devices or in the memory hardware. The operating system constantly needs to be aware of possible errors. It should take the appropriate action to ensure correct and consistent computing.

Operating system with multiple users provides following services.

1. Resource Allocation.
2. Accounting.
3. Protection.

A) Resource Allocation

If there are more than one user or jobs running at the same time, then resources must be allocated to each of them. Operating system manages different types of resources require special allocation code, i.e. main memory, CPU cycles and file storage.

There are some resources which require only general request and release code. For allocating CPU, CPU scheduling algorithms are used for better utilization of CPU. CPU scheduling algorithms are used for better utilization of CPU. CPU scheduling routines consider the speed of the CPU, number of available registers and other required factors.

B) Accounting

Logs of each user must be kept. It is also necessary to keep record of which user how much and what kinds of computer resources. This log is used for accounting purposes. The accounting data may be used for statistics or for the billing. It also used to improve system efficiency.

C) Protection

Protection involves ensuring that all access to system resources is controlled. Security starts with each user having to authenticate to the system, usually by means of a password. External I/O devices must be also protected from invalid access attempts.

In protection, all the access to the resources is controlled. In multiprocess environment, it is possible that, one process to interface with the other, or with the operating system, so protection is required.

User Operating System Interface - CLI

- Command Line Interface (CLI) or command interpreter allows direct command entry.
- Sometimes implemented in kernel, sometimes by systems program.
- Sometimes multiple flavours implemented – shells.
- Primarily fetches a command from user and executes it.
- Sometimes commands built-in, sometimes just names of programs.
- If the latter, adding new features doesn't require shell modification.

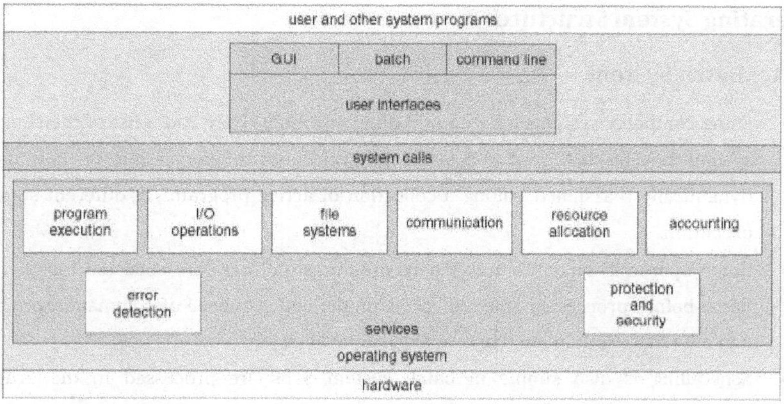

User Operating System Interface - GUI

- User-friendly desktop metaphor interface.
- Usually mouse, keyboard, and monitor.
- Icons represent files, programs, actions, etc.
- Various mouse buttons over objects in the interface cause various actions (provide information, options, execute function, open directory (known as a folder).
- Invented at Xerox PARC.
- Many systems now include both CLI and GUI interfaces.
- Microsoft Windows is GUI with CLI "command" shell.
- Apple Mac OS X as "Aqua" GUI interface with UNIX kernel underneath and shells available.
- Solaris is CLI with optional GUI interfaces (Java Desktop, KDE).

1.10. Operating System Components

Modern operating systems share the goal of supporting the system components. The system components are :

1. Process Management.
2. Main Memory Management.
3. File Management.
4. Secondary Storage Management.
5. I/O System Management.
6. Networking.
7. Protection System.
8. Command Interpreter System.

Operating System Structures

1.11. Batch System

- Some computer systems only do one thing at a time. They had a list of the computer system may be dedicated to a single program until its completion, or they may be dynamically reassigned among a collection of active programs in different stages of execution.
- Batch operating system is one where programs and data are collected together in a batch before processing starts. A job is predefined sequence of commands, programs and data that are combined in to a single unit called job.
- Scheduling is also simple in batch system. Jobs are processed in the order of submission i.e first come first served fashion.
- When job completed execution, its memory is releases and the output for the job gets copied into an output spool for later printing.
- Batch system often provides simple forms of file management. Access to file is serial. Batch systems do not require any time critical device management.
- Batch systems are inconvenient for users because users can not interact with their jobs to fix problems. There may also be long turn around times.
- Example of this system id generating monthly bank statement.

Advantages of Batch System:

- Move much of the work of the operator to the computer.
- Increased performance since it was possible for job to start as soon as the previous job finished.

Disadvantages of Batch System:

- Turn around time can be large from user standpoint.
- Difficult to debug program.
- A job could enter an infinite loop.
- A job could corrupt the monitor, thus affecting pending jobs.
- Due to lack of protection scheme, one batch job can affect pending jobs.

1.12. Time Sharing Systems

- Multi-programmed batched systems provide an environment where the various system resources (for example, CPU, memory, peripheral devices) are utilized effectively.

- Time-sharing or multi-tasking, is a logical extension of multiprogramming. Multiple jobs are executed by the CPU switvching between them, but the switches occur so frequently that the users may interact with each program while it is running.
- An interactive, or hands-on, computer ssytem provides online communication between the user and the system. The user gives instructions to the operating system or to program directly, and receives an immediate response. Usually, a keyboard is used to provide input, and a display screen is used as a Monitor.
- If users are to be able to access both data and code conveniently, an on-line file system must be available. A file is a collection of related information defined by its creator. Batch systems are appropriate for executing large jobs that need little interaction.
- A time-shared operating system allows the many users to share the computer simultaneously. Since each action or command in a time-shared system tends to be short, only a little CPU time is needed for each user. As the system switches rapidly from one user to the next, each user is given the impression that she has her own computer, whereas actually one computer is being shared among many users.
- Time-sharing operating systems are even more complex than are multi-programmed operating systems. As in multiprogramming, several jobs must be kept simultaneously in memory, which requires some form of memory management and protection.
- Time-sharing systems were developed to provide interactive use of a computer system at a reasonable cost. A time-shared operating system uses CPU scheduling and multiprogramming to provide each user with a small portion of a time-shared computer. Each user has at least one separate program in memory. A program that is loaded into memory and is executing is commonly referred to as a process. When a process executes, it typically executes for only a short time before it either finishes or needs to perform I/O. I/O may be interactive; that is, output is to a display for the user and input is from a user keyboard. Since interactive I/O typically runs at people speeds, it may take a long time to completed.

1.13. Multiprogramming

- When two or more programs are in memory at the same time, sharing the processor is referred to the multiprogramming operating system. Multiprogramming assumes a single processor that is being shared. It increases CPU utilization by organizing jobs so that the CPU always has one to execute.
- Fig. 1.2 shows the memory layout for a multiprogramming system.

- The operating system keeps several jobs in memory at a time. This set of jobs is a subset of the jobs kept in the job pool. The operating system picks and begins to execute one of the jobs in the memory.
- Multi-programmed system provide with an environment in which the various system resources are utilized effectively, but they do not provide for user interaction with the computer system.
- Jobs entering into the system are kept into the memory. Operating system picks the job and begins to execute one of the jobs in the memory. Havingseveral programs in memory at the same time requires some form of memory management.

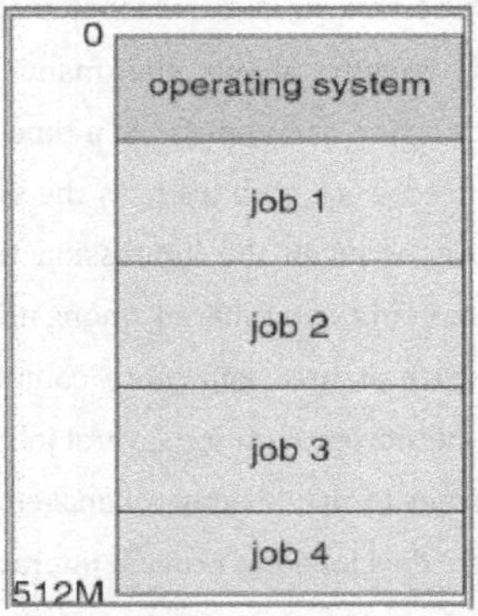

Advantages

1. High CPU utilization.
2. It appears that many programs are allotted CPU almost simultaneously.

Disadvantages

- CPU scheduling is required.
- To accommodate many jobs in memory, memory management is required.

1.14. Spooling

- Acronym for simultaneous peripheral operations on line. Spooling refers to putting jobs in a buffer, a special area in memory or on a disk where a device can access them when it is ready.
- Spooling is useful because device access data that different rates. The buffer provides a waiting station where data can rest while the slower device catches up. Fig 2.3 shows the spooling.

- Computer can perform I/O in parallel with computation, it becomes possible to have the computer read a deck of cards to a tape, drum or disk and to write out to a tape printer while it was computing. This process is called spooling.
- The most common spooling application is print spooling. In print spooling, documents are loaded into a buffer and then the printer pulls them off the buffer at its own rate.
- Spooling is also used for processing data at remote sites. The CPU sends the data via communications path to a remote printer. Spooling overlaps the I/O of one job with the computation of other jobs.
- One difficulty with simple batch systems is that the computer still needs to read the decks of cards before it can begin to execute the job. This means that the CPU is idle during these relatively slow operations.
- Spooling batch systems were the first and are the simplest of the multiprogramming systems.

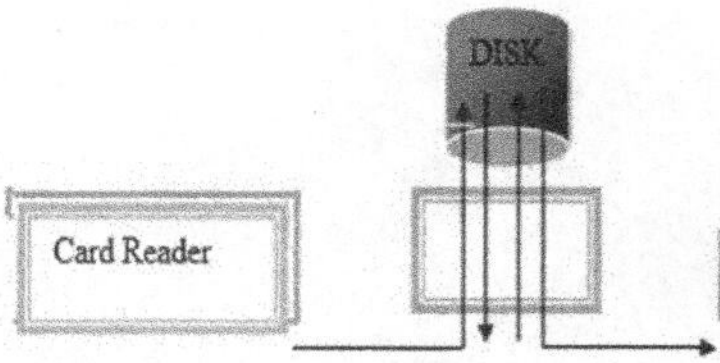

Spooling Process

Advantage of Spooling

- The spooling operation uses a disk as a very large buffer.
- Spooling is however capable of overlapping I/O operation for one job with processor operations for another job.

1.15. Essential Properties of the Operating System

1. **Batch:** Jobs with similar needs are batched together and run through the computer as a group by an operator or automatic job sequencer. Performance is increased by attempting to keep CPU and I/O devices busy at all times through buffering , off line operation, spooling and multiprogramming. A Batch system is good for executing large jobs that need little interaction, it can be submitted and picked up later.
2. **Time sharing:** Uses CPU scheduling and multiprogramming to provide economical interactive use of a system. The CPU switches rapidly from one user to another i.e. the CPU is shared between a number of interactive users. Instead of having a job defined by spooled card images, each program reads its next control instructions from the terminal and output is normally printed immediately on the screen.

3. **Interactive:** User is on line with computer system and interacts with it via an interface. It is typically composed of many short transactions where the result of the next transaction may be unpredictable. Response time needs to be short since the user submits and waits for the result.
4. **Real time system:** Real time systems are usually dedicated, embedded systems. They typically read from and react to sensor data. The system must generate response to events within fixed periods of time to ensure correct performance.
5. **Distributed:** Distributes computation among several physical processors. The processors do not share memory or a clock. Instead, each processor has its own local memory. Then communicate with each other through various communication lines.

1.16. System Calls

Types of System Calls

- Process control
- File management
- Device management
- Information maintenance
- Communications
- Protection

Examples of System Calls

	Windows	Unix
Process Control	CreateProcess() ExitProcess() WaitForSingleObject()	fork() exit() wait()
File Manipulation	CreateFile() ReadFile() WriteFile() CloseHandle()	open() read() write() close()
Device Manipulation	SetConsoleMode() ReadConsole() WriteConsole()	ioctl() read() write()
Information Maintenance	GetCurrentProcessID() SetTimer() Sleep()	getpid() alarm() sleep()
Communication	CreatePipe() CreateFileMapping() MapViewOfFile()	pipe() shmget() mmap()
Protection	SetFileSecurity() InitlializeSecurityDescriptor() SetSecurityDescriptorGroup()	chmod() umask() chown()

1.17. System Program

System programs provide a convenient environment for program development and execution. The can be divided into:

- File manipulation
- Status information
- File modification
- Programming language support
- Program loading and execution
- Communications
- Application programs

Most users' view of the operation system is defined by system programs, not the actual system calls.

- Provide a convenient environment for program development and execution.
- Some of them are simply user interfaces to system calls; others are considerably more complex.
- File management - Create, delete, copy, rename, print, dump, list, and generally manipulate files and directories.
- Status information.
- Some ask the system for info - date, time, amount of available memory, disk space, number of users.
- Others provide detailed performance, logging, and debugging information.
- Typically, these programs format and print the output to the terminal or other output devices.
- Some systems implement a registry - used to store and retrieve configuration information.

1.18. Linux introduction and File System

Linux looks like UNIX system. Linux is developed by Linux Torvalds. Linux development began in 1991. Linux source code is available for free on the internet. The basic Linux system is standard environment for applications and use programming.

1.18.1. Components of a Linux System

Any Linux system consists of three components.

1. Kernel
2. System libraries
3. System utilities

Kernel

The Kernel is responsible for maintaining all the important abstraction of the operating system. It includes virtual memory and processes. Kernel is most important component of the Linux system. It contains standard set of functions through which application can interact with the Kernel. System library implements much of the operating system functionality that does not need the full privileges of Kernel code.

System Utilities

System utilities are programs that perform individual, specialized management tasks.

System Management programs	User Processes	User utility programs	Compilers
System shared libraries			
Linux Kernel			
Loadable Kernel modules			

- Fig. shows the components of the Linux system.
- All the Kernel code executes in the processors privileged mode with full access to all the physical resources of the computer. Linux refers to this privileged mode as Kernel mode. In Linux, no user mode code is built into the Kernel.

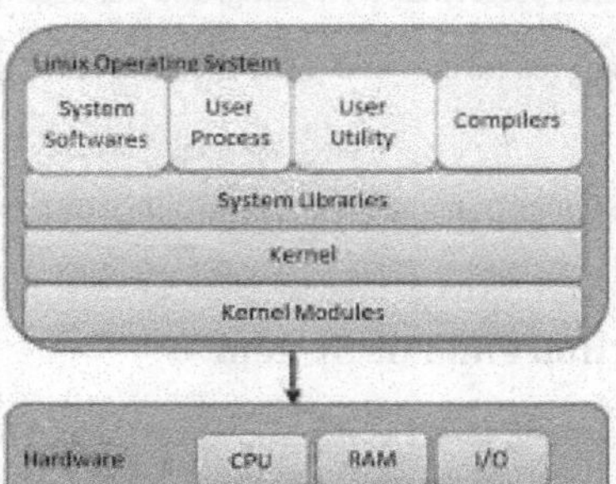

Components of Linux system

- Any operating system support code that does not need to run in Kernel mode is placed into the system libraries instead.
- The Kernel is created as a single, monolithic binary. All Kernel code and data structures are kept in a single address space, no context switches are necessary when a process calls an operating system function. Core scheduling, virtual memory code also occupied same address space.
- Linux Kernel provides all the functionality necessary to run processes, and it provides system services to give arbitrated and protected access to hardware resources
- The Linux system includes a wide variety of user mode programs both system utilities and user utilities.

1.19. Kernel Modules

- Kernel code executes in Kernel mode with full access to all the physical resources of the computer. Sections of Kernel code that can be compiled, loaded and unloaded independent of the rest of the Kernel.
- Kernel module may typically implement a device driver, a file system, or a networking protocol. The module interface allows third parties to write and distribute, on their own teams, device drivers or file systems that could not be distributed under the GPL.
- The loadable Kernel modules run in privileged Kernel mode. Kernel modules allow a Linux system to be setup with a standard, minimal Kernel, without any extra device drivers built in. Kernel management allows modules to be dynamically loaded into memory when needed.
- Linux Kernel modules has three components.
    1. Module management.
    2. Driver registration.
    3. Conflict resolution mechanism.

1. Module management

1. It support loading modules into memory and letting them talk to the rest of the Kernel.
2. Linux maintains an internal symbol table in the Kernel.
3. Module loading is split into two separate sections:
    a) Managing sections of module code in Kernel memory.
    b) Handling symbols that modules are allowed to reference.
4. Symbol table does not contain the full set of symbol defined in the Kernel during latter compilation.

5. The module requestor manages loading requested, but currently unloaded modules.
6. It also regularly queries the Kernel to see whether a dynamically loaded module is still in use and will unload it when it is no longer actively needed.
7. Original service request will complete once the module is loaded.

2. Driver Registration

1. Allows modules to tell the rest of the kernel that a new driver has become available.
2. Kernel maintains dynamic tables of all known drivers.
3. Kernel also provides a set of routines to allow drivers to be added or removed.
4. Registration table contains following:
   a) Device drivers
   b) File systems
   c) Network protocols
   d) Binary format.
5. Device drivers may be block or character devices.
6. Files system contains network file system, virtual file system etc.
7. Network protocol includes IPX, packet filtering rules for a network.

3. Conflict Resolution

1. A mechanisms that allows different device drivers to reserve hardware resources and to protect those resources from accidental use by another driver.
2. Linux provides a ventral conflict resolution mechanism.
3. Conflict resolution module aims are:
   a) To prevent modules from clashing over access to hardware resources.
   b) Prevent auto probes from interfering with existing device drivers.
   c) Resolve conflicts among multiple drivers trying to access the same hardware.
4. Kernel maintains lists of allocated hardware resources.

1.20. Basic Features

UNIX has a number of features, mostly good and some bad, but it is necessary to know at least some of them:

1. ***UNIX is Portable:*** Portability is the ability of the software that operates on one machine to operate on another, different machine. In UNIX there are two types of portability, that of the UNIX operating system itself (i.e. the Kernel program) and of the application program.

Advantages of portability are:

a) Portable application program decrease the programming costs.

b) Retraining is avoided as the end user works on a similar system with enhanced capabilities.

2. ***Open system:*** The system that more than one system can access the same data at the same time. Several people involved in a common project can conveniently access each other's data. Apart from data, other resources like memory (RAM), the CPU(the chip), or the hard disk can be used by many users simultaneously.
3. ***Multi-user Capability:*** This means that more than one system can access the same data at the same time. Several people involved in a common project can conveniently access each other's data. Apart from data, other resources like memory(RAM), the CPU(the chip), or the hard disk can be used by many users simultaneously.
4. ***Multi-tasking Capability:*** Multi-tasking means that a user can perform more than one tasks at the same time. A user can do this by placing some tasks in the background while he works on a task in the foreground. An ampersand(&) placed at the end of the command line sends the process in background.
5. ***Hierarchical File System***: Hierarchical structure offers maximum flexibility for grouping information in a way that reflects in natural structure. The programs and data can be organized conveniently since files can be grouped according to usage.
6. ***The shell:*** User interaction with UNIX is controlled by the shell, a powerful command interpreter. The shell has various capabilities like redirecting the application input and output and also to progress a group of files with a single command.
7. ***UNIX has built in networking:*** The UNIX has various built in programs and utilities like UUCP, mail, write, etc. With these utilities one can communicate with other user or one server to another.
8. ***Security***: Computer system security means protecting hardware and the information contained within the system. Security means to avoid:

a) Unauthorized access to the computer system.

b) Unauthorized examination of output.

c) Unauthorized tapping of data.

d) Destruction of software data by mistake or on purpose.

e) Examination of sensitive data by unauthorized users and alteration of sensitive data without detection.

The UNIX provides the features like:

a) Password protection for system access.

b) Control access to individual files.

c) Encryption of data files.

9. ***Software Development Tools:*** UNIX offers an excellent variety of tools for software development for all phases, from program editing to maintenance of software.

1.21. Basic Architecture of UNIX/LINUX System

The figure shows the architecture of the UNIX system in the form of various layers. The inner most layer i.e. core is the hardware of the computer system. The kernel is a software which directly comes in contact with the hardware and controls the hardware. A layer above this is the shell.

Above this the various utilities like nroff, troff, vi, as, etc. and the various compilers and other application program reside. Let us see these layers and their functions in detail:

1. **Hardware:** The hardware at the centre of the structure provides the operatingsystem with basic services. The hardware constitutes all the peripherals like memory (RAM, HDD, FDD, CD etc), processor, mouse and other input devices, terminal (i.e. VDUs), printers etc.

2. **The Kernel:** The operating system interacts directly with the hardware, providing common services to programs and insulating user program complexities of hardware. The operating system is also called as Kernel. This kernel interacts directly with the hardware. Because of this hardware isolation of user program, it is easy to move the user programs easily between UNIX systems running on different hardware.

3. **Shell:** Shell is actually the interface between the user and the Kernel that isolates the user from knowledge of Kernel functions. The shell accepts the commands keyed in by the users and checks for their syntax and gives out error messages if something goes. These command after getting interpreted by the shell are provided to kernel for appropriate action. It also provides the features of pipe (|) and redirection (i.e. <, >, >>, <<). The shell also has a programming capability of **its** own. There are a number of shells available in various UNIX flavours but common are.

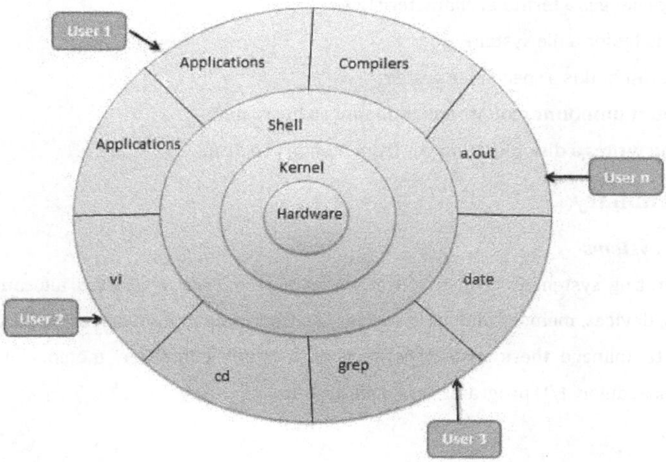

Architecture of UNIX System

a) Bourne Shell (sh)

b) C Shell (csh)

c) Korn Shell (ksh)

The other shells are: bash, restricted Shell(rsh) and visual Shell(vsh). The bourne Shell (sh) is also called a standard shell.

4. **UNIX utilities:** The UNIX system Kernel does only level jobs necessary to schedule processes, keep track of files, and control hardware devices.

All other operating system functions are done by utility programs written assoftware tools. Following are some of the utilities that play a prominent role in the operating of the UNIX system.

a) **Init** initializes the process creation mechanism. For each terminal where a login is allowed, init creates a process that prints the login: message.

b) **Getty process** –conditions|| the connection to the terminal so that the terminal can communicate with the computer and then prints the login: message.

c) **Login** when an user responds to the login prompt the login program replaces getty. If the user account has a password, login prints the password : message and checks to see that the password entered is correct. If correct, program named in password file, usually Bourne shell or C shell replaces login and the user is successfully logged into the system.

d) **stty** changes a terminal characteristics.

e) **mkfs** builds a file system.

f) **mknod** builds a special file system.

g) **mount unmount** mounts and unmounts a file system.

h) **syne** writes a disk block images from memory to disk.

1.22. Summary

Operating Systems

An operating system is always concerned with resources & services allocation such as processors, devices, memory and information. The Operating System correspondingly includes programs to manage these resources, such as a traffic controller, memory management module, a scheduler, I/O programs, and a file system.

Assembler

Input to an assembler is an assembly language program. Output is an object program and the information that enables the loader to prepare the object program for the execution.

Compiler

Compiler is a program or combination of processes which can accept a source program in a user-friendly language and produces a corresponding Source code or object program. An Interpreter is a program that seems to execute a source code as a machine language.

Loader

The loader generally loads, relocates and links the object program. Loader is a program that relocates the programs into the memory and prepares them for execution.

Linux is a modern, free operating system based on UNIX standards. It has designed to run efficiently and reliably on common PC hardware; it also runs on a variety of other platforms. It provide a programming interface and user interface compatible with standard UNIX systems and can run a large number of UNIX applications, including an increasing number of commercially supported applications.

Linux has not evolved in a vacuum a completely Linux system includes many components that were developed independently of Linux. The core Linux operating system kernel is entirely original, but allows much existing free UNIX software to run, resulting in a entire UNIX compatible operating system free from proprietary code. The Linux kernel is implemented as a traditional monolithic kernel for performance reasons, but it is modular enough in design to allow most drivers to be dynamically loaded and unloaded at run time.

1.23. Model Questions

1. Define Operating System?
2. Explain various function of operating system?
3. Explain I/O system Management?
4. Define & explain Assembler, Loader, Compiler?
5. Explain various operating system services?
6. Define Spooling? Describe Spooling process?
7. Differentiate Multitasking & Multiprogramming?
8. List different components of a linux system?
9. What are Kernel modules?
10. Explain Basic architecture of UNIX/Linux system?
11. Explain basic features of UNIX/Linux?
12. Define and explain Shell?

1.24. Objective Questions

1. An operating system acts as a ____________ between a user of a system and the system's hardware. **(Interface, Intermediary)**
2. The process that is always under the execution state is known as __________. **(Kernel)**
3. The main functions of an operating system are ______, _________ and ________. **(Convenience, Efficiency, Ability to evolve)**
4. The hardware of a computer consists of ____________. **(memory, CPU, ALU, I/O Devices, Peripheral device and storage device)**
5. System program comprises of ___________. **(Compilers, loaders, OS, editors).**
6. The primary objective of the Operating system is __________. **(Resource allocation)**
7. The module which keeps track of the device status is known as the__________. **(I/O traffic controller)**
8. __________ is a program or combination of processes which can accept a source program in a user-friendly language and produces a corresponding Source code or object program. **(Compiler)**
9. An __________ is a program that seems to execute a source code as a machine language. **(Interpreter)**
10. ____________ is a kind of routine that loads an object program and gets it ready for execution. **(Loader)**

11. An __________ provides services to programs and to those users individually for each program. **(operating system)**

12. ____________ is one of the services provided by the Operating system. **(Program Execution, File system Manipulation, Communications, I/O Operations, Error detection)**

13. Communication can be done by _________ and __________. **(Message passing, Shared memory)**

14. _________ is the processing principle for Batch processing system. **(First come first serve)**

15. __________________ is a logical extension of multiprogramming **(Time-sharing or multitasking)**

16. When two or more programs are in memory at the same time, sharing the processor is referred to the __________ operating system. **(multiprogramming)**

17. _______ operating system is one where programs and data are collected together in a batch before processing starts. **(Batch)**

18. A _________ is good for executing large jobs that need little interaction, it can be submitted and picked up later. **(Batch system)**

19. The spooling operation uses a _____ as a very large buffer. **(disk)**

20. ___________ is the most common spooling application. **(Print spooling)**

21. Which command is used to set terminal IO characteristic?

    a) tty

    b) ctty

    c) ptty

    d) sty

22. The dmesg command

    a) Shows user login logoff attempts.

    b) Shows the syslog file for info messages

    c) Kernel log messages

    d) Shows the daemon log messages

23. The command “mknodmyfifo b 4 16”

    a) Will create a block device if user is root

    b) Will create a block device for all users

    c) Will create a FIFO if user is not root

    d) None of the mentioned

24. Which command is used to display the operating system name

    a) os

    b) unix

    c) kernel

    d) uname

25. Which command is used to record a user login session in a file

    a) macro

    b) read

    c) script

    d) none of the mentioned

26. Which command is used to print a file

    a) print

    b) ptr

    c) lpr

    d) none of the mentioned

27. Which option of ls command used to view file inode number

    a) –l

    b) –o

    c) –a

    d) –i

28. Using which command you find resource limits to the session?

    a) rlimit

    b) ulimit

    c) setrlimit

    d) getrlimit

29. Find / -name '*' will

    a) List all files and directories recursively starting from /

    b) List a file named * in /

    c) List all files in / directory

    d) List all files and directories in / directory

30. Which command is used to display the unix version.

    a) uname -r

    b) uname –n

    c) uname –t

    d) kernel

CHAPTER 2

CPU & PROCESS SCHEDULING

2.1. Objectives

After going through this unit, you will be able to:

- To introduce the notion of a process – a program in execution, which forms the basis of all computation
- To describe the various features of processes, including scheduling, creation and termination, and communication.
- To introduce the concurrency control and Race condition, critical section problem, where solutions can be used to ensure the consistency of shared data.
- To present both software and hardware solutions of the critical section problem.
- To introduce Thread & its types, Multithreading Models and Threading issues.

2.2. Concept of Process

- A process is sequential program in execution. A process defines the fundamental unit of computation for the computer. Components of process are:
    1. Object program.
    2. Data.
    3. Resources.
    4. Status of the process examination.
- Object program i.e. code to be executed. Data is used for executing the program. While executing the program, it may require some resources. Last component is used for verifying the status of the process execution. A process can run to completion only when all requested resources have been allocated to the process. Two or more processes could be executing the same program, each using their own data and resources.

2.2.1. Processes and Programs

- Process is a dynamic entity that is a program in execution. A process is a sequence of information executions. Process exists in a limited span of time. Two or more processes could be executing the same program, each using their own data and resources.
- Program is a static entity made up of program statement. Program contains the instructions. A program exists at single place in space and continues to exist. A program does not perform the action by itself.

2.3. Process State

- When process executes, it changes state. Process state is defined as the current activity of the process. Fig. 2.1 shows the general form of the process state transition diagram. Process state contains five states. Each process is in one of the states. The states are listed below.
    1. New
    2. Ready
    3. Running
    4. Waiting
    5. Terminating (exit)

1. New: A process that just been created.
2. Ready: Ready processes are waiting to have the processor allocated to them by the operating system so that they can run.
3. Running: The process that is currently being executed. A running process possesses all the resources needed for its execution, including the processor.
4. Waiting: A process that cannot execute until some event occurs such as the completion of an I/O operation. The running process may become suspended by invoking an I/O module.
5. Terminated: A process that has been released from the pool of executable processes by the operating system.

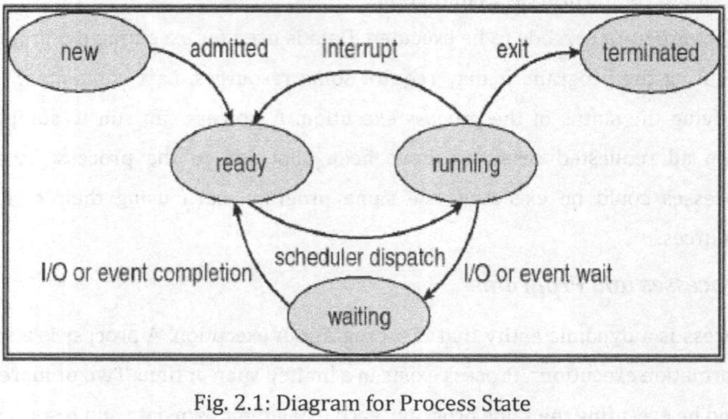

Fig. 2.1: Diagram for Process State

- Whenever processes changes state, the operating system reacts by placing the process PCB in the list that corresponds to its new state. Only oneprocess can be running on any processor at any instant and many processes may be ready and waiting state.

2.3.1. Suspended Processes

Characteristics of suspend process.

1. Suspended process is not immediately available for execution.
2. The process may or may not be waiting on an event.
3. For preventing the execution, process is suspended by OS, parent process, process itself and an agent.
4. Process may not be removed from the suspended state until the agent orders the removal.
   - Swapping is used to move all of a process from main memory to disk. When all the process by putting it in the suspended state and transferring it to disk.

Reasons for process suspension.

1. Swapping.
2. Timing.
3. Interactive user request.
4. Parent process request.

Swapping: OS needs to release required main memory to bring in a process that is ready to execute.

Timing: Process may be suspended while waiting for the next time interval.

Interactive user request: Process may be suspended for debugging purpose by user.

Parent process request: To modify the suspended process or to coordinate the activity of various descendants.

2.3.2. Process Control Block (PCB)

- Each process contains the process control block (PCB). PCB is the data structure used by the operating system. Operating system groups all information that needs about particular process. Fig. 2.2 shows the process control block.

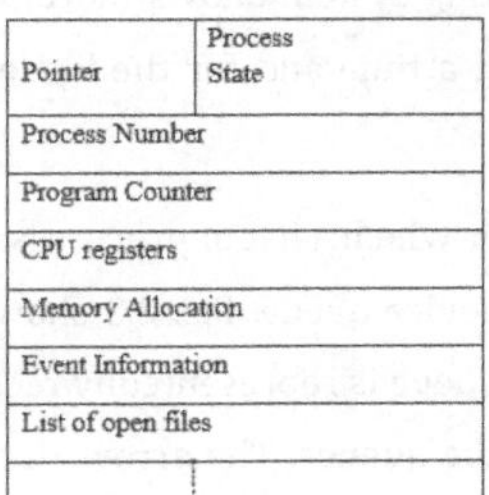

Fig. 2.2: Process Control Block

1. Pointer: Pointer points to another process control block. Pointer is used for maintaining the scheduling list.
2. Process State: Process state may be new, ready, running, waiting and so on.
3. Program Counter: It indicates the address of the next instruction to be executed for this process.
4. Event information: For a process in the blocked state this field contains information concerning the event for which the process is waiting.
5. CPU register: It indicates general purpose register, stack pointers, index registers and accumulators, etc. number of register and type of register totally depends upon the computer architecture.
6. Memory Management Information: This information may include the value of base and limit register. This information is useful for de-allocating the memory when the process terminates.
7. Accounting Information: This information includes the amount of CPU and real time, used time limits, job or process numbers, account numbers etc.

- Process control block also includes the information about CPU scheduling, I/O resource management, file management information, priority and so on.
- When a process is created, hardware registers and flags are set to the values provided by the loader or linker. Whenever that process is suspended, the contents of the processor register are usually saved on the stack and the pointer to the related stack frame is stored in the PCB. In this way, the hardware state can be restored when the process is scheduled to run again.

2.4. Process Management / Process Scheduling

- Multiprogramming operating system allows more than one process to be loaded into the executable memory at a time and for the loaded process to share the CPU using time multiplexing.
- Device queue is a queue for which a list of processes waiting for a particular I/O device. Each device has its own device queue. Fig. 2.3 shows the queuing diagram of process scheduling. In the fig 2.3, queue is representedby rectangular box. The circles represent the resources that serve the queues. The arrows indicate the flow of processes in the system.

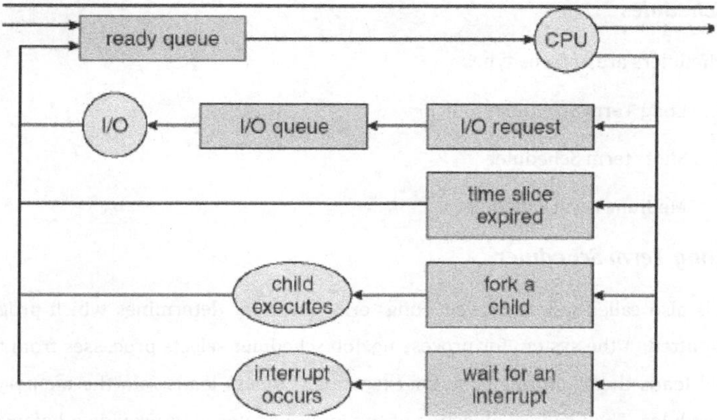

Fig. 2.3: Queue Diagram of Process Scheduling

- **Queues are of two types:** ready queue and set of device queues. A newly arrived process is put in the ready queue. Processes are waiting in ready queue for allocating the CPU. Once the CPU is assigned to the process, then process will execute. While executing the process, one of the several events could occur.

1. The process could issue an I/O request and then place in an I/O queue.
2. The process could create new sub process and waits for its termination.
3. The process could be removed forcibly from the CPU, as a result of interrupt and put back in the ready queue.

2.4.1. *Two State Process Model*

- Process may be in one of two states:
  a) Running
  b) Not Running
- When new process is created by OS that process enters into the system in the running state.
- Processes that are not running are kept in queue, waiting their turn to execute. Each entry in the queue is a printer to a particular process. Queue is implemented by using linked list. Use of dispatcher is as follows. When a process interrupted, that process is transferred in the waiting queue. If the process has completed or aborted, the process is discarded. In either case, the dispatcher then selects a process from the queue to execute.

2.4.2. Schedules

- Schedulers are of three types.
  1. Long Term Scheduler
  2. Short term Scheduler
  3. Medium Term Scheduler

2.4.2.1. Long Term Scheduler

- It is also called job scheduler. Long term scheduler determines which programs are admitted to the system for processing. Job scheduler selects processes from the queue and loads them into memory for execution. Process loads into the memory for CPU scheduler. The primary objective of the job scheduler is to provide a balanced mix of jobs, such as I/O bound and processor bound. It also controls the degree of multiprogramming. If the degree of multiprogramming is stable, then the average rate of process creation must be equal to the average departure rate of processes leaving the system.
- On same systems, the long-term scheduler may be absent or minimal. Time-sharing operating systems have no long-term scheduler. When process changes the state from new to ready, then there is a long-term scheduler.

2.4.2.2. Short Term Scheduler

- It is also called CPU scheduler. Main objective is increasing system performance in accordance with the chosen set of criteria. It is the change of ready state to running state of the process. CPU scheduler selects from among the processes that are ready to execute and allocates the CPU to one of them.
- Short term scheduler also known as dispatcher, execute most frequently and makes the fine-grained decision of which process to execute next. Short term scheduler is faster than long tern scheduler.

2.4.2.3. Medium Term Scheduler

- Medium term scheduling is part of the swapping function. It removes the processes from the memory. It reduces the degree of multiprogramming. The medium-term scheduler is in charge of handling the swapped out-processes.

Medium term scheduler is shown in the Fig. 2.4.

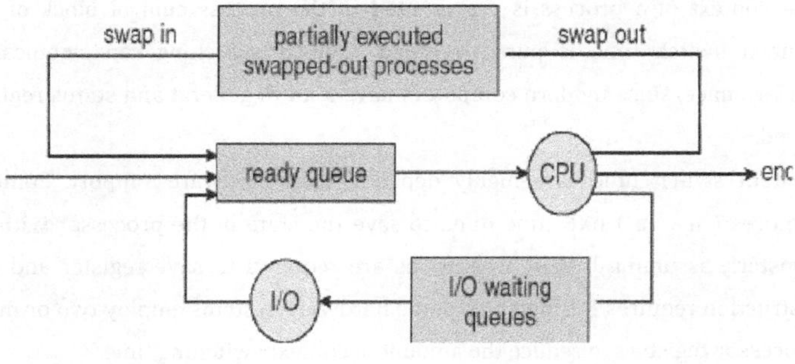

Fig. 2.4: Queuing Diagram with Medium Term Scheduler

Running process may become suspended by making an I/O request. Suspended processes cannot make any progress towards completion. In this condition, to remove the process from memory and make space for other process. Suspended process is move to the secondary storage is called swapping, and the process is said to be swapped out or rolled out. Swapping may be necessary to improve the process mix.

2.4.2.4. Comparison between Scheduler

Sr. No.	*Long Term*	*Short Term*	*Medium Term*
1	*It is job scheduler*	*It is CPU Scheduler*	*It is swapping*
2	*Speed is less than short term scheduler*	*Speed is very fast*	*Speed is in between both*
3	*It controls degree of multiprogramming*	*Less control over degree of multiprogramming*	*Reduce the degree of multiprogramming.*
4	*Absent or minimal in time sharing system.*	*Minimal in time sharing system.*	*Time sharing system use medium term scheduler.*
5	*It select processes from pool and load them into memory for execution.*	*It select from among the processes that are ready to execute.*	*Process can be reintroduced into memory and its execution can be continued.*
6	*Process state is (New to Ready)*	*Process state is (Ready to Running)*	-
7	*Select a good process, mix of I/O bound and CPU bound.*	*Select a new process for a CPU quite frequently.*	-

2.5 Context Switch

- When the scheduler switches the CPU from executing one process to executing another, the context switcher saves the content of all processor registers for the process being removed from the CPU in its process being removed from the CPU in its process descriptor.

The context of a process is represented in the process control block of a process. Context switch time is pure overhead. Context switching can significantly affect performance, since modern computers have a lot of general and status registers to be saved.

- Content switch times are highly dependent on hardware support. Context switch requires (n + m) bXK time units to save the state of the processor with n general registers, assuming b store operations are required to save register and each store instruction requires K time units. Some hardware systems employ two or more sets of processor registers to reduce the amount of context switching time.
- When the process is switched the information stored is:
    1. Program Counter
    2. Scheduling Information
    3. Base and limit register value
    4. Currently used register
    5. Changed State
    6. I/O State
    7. Accounting

2.6. Operation on Processes

- Several operations are possible on the process. Process must be created and deleted dynamically. Operating system must provide the environment for the process operation. We discuss the two main operations on processes.

2.6.1. Create Process

- Operating system creates a new process with the specified or default attributes and identifier. A process may create several new sub processes. Syntax for creating new process is:

CREATE (processed, attributes)

- Two names are used in the process they are parent process and child process. Parent process is a creating process. Child process is created by the parent process. Child process may create another sub process. So it forms a tree of processes. When operating system issues a CREATE system call, it obtains a new process control block from the pool of free memory, fills the fields with provided and default parameters, and insert the PCB into the ready list. Thus, it makes the specified process eligible to run the process.

- When a process is created, it requires some parameters. These are priority, level of privilege, requirement of memory, access right, memory protection information etc. Process will need certain resources, such as CPU time, memory, files and I/O devices to complete the operation. When process creates a subprocess, that subprocess may obtain its resources directly from the operating system. Otherwise it uses the resources of parent process.
- When a process creates a new process, two possibilities exist in terms of execution.
    1. The parent continues to execute concurrently with its children.
    2. The parent waits until some or all of its children have terminated.
- For address space, two possibilities occur:
    1. The child process is a duplicate of the parent process.
    2. The child process has a program loaded into it.

2.6.2. Terminate a Process

- DELETE system call is used for terminating a process. A process may delete itself or by another process. A process can cause the termination of another process via an appropriate system call. The operating system reacts by reclaiming all resources allocated to the specified process, closing files opened by or for the process. PCB is also removed from its place of residence in the list and is returned to the free pool. The DELETE service is normally invoked as a part of orderly program termination.
- Following are the resources for terminating the child process by parent process.
    1. The task given to the child is no longer required.
    2. Child has exceeded its usage of some of the resources that it has been allocated.
    3. Operating system does not allow a child to continue if its parent terminates.

2.7. Co-Operating Processes

- Co-operating process is a process that can affect or be affected by the other processes while executing. If suppose any process is sharing data with other processes, then it is called co-operating process. Benefit of the co-operating processes are:
    1. Sharing of information.
    2. Increases computation speed.
    3. Modularity.
    4. Convenience.

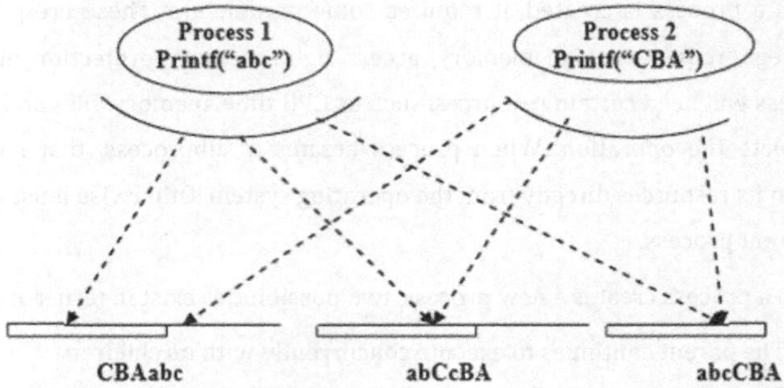

- Co-operating processes share the information: Such as a file, memory etc. System must provide an environment to allow concurrent access to these types of resources. Computation speed will increase if the computer has multiple processing elements are connected together. System is constructed in a modular fashion. System function is divided into number of modules.
- Behaviour of co-operating processes is nondeterministic i.e. it depends on relative execution sequence and cannot be predicted a priori. Co-operating processes are also Reproducible. For example, suppose one process writes –ABC||, another writes –CBA|| can get different outputs, cannot tell what comes from which. Which process output first –C|| in –ABCCBA||. The subtle state sharing that occurs here via the terminal. Not just anything can happen, though. For example, –AABBCC|| cannot occur.

2.8. Process Scheduling & Principle of Concurrency

1. In a single-processor multiprogramming system, processes are interleaved in time to yield the appearance of simultaneous execution. Even parallel processing is not achieved, and ever though there is a certain amount of overhead involved in switching back and forth between processes, interleaved execution provides major benefits in processing efficiency and in program structuring. In a multiple processor system, it is possible not only to interleave the execution of multiple processes but also to overlap them. It is assumed, it may seem that interleaving and overlapping represent fundamentally different modes of execution and present different problems. In fact, both techniques can be viewed as examples of concurrent processing, and both present the same problems. The relative speed of execution of processes It depends on activities of other processes, the way in which the operating system handles interrupts, and the scheduling policies of the operating, system.

   There are quite difficulties:

1. The sharing of global resources. For example, if two processes both make use of the same global variable and both perform reads and writes on that variable, then the order in which the various reads and writes are executed is critical.
2. It is difficult for the operating system to manage the allocation of resources optimally.
3. It is very difficult to locate a programming error because results are typically not deterministic and reproducible.

Ex

```
Void echo()
{
chin = getchar();
chout = chin;
putchar(chout);
}
```

This procedure shows the essential elements of a program that will provide a character echo procedure; input is obtained from a keyboard one keystroke at a time. Each input character is stored in variable chin. It is then transferred to variable chout and sent to the display. Any program can call this procedure repeatedly to accept user input and display it on the user's screen.

In a single - processor multiprogramming system supporting a single user. The user can jump from one application to another, and each .application uses the same keyboard for input and the same screen for output. Because each application needs to use the procedure echo, it makes sense for it to be a shared procedure that is loaded into a portion of memory global to all applications. Thus, only a single copy of the echo procedure is used, saving space.

The sharing of main memory among processes is useful to permit efficient and close interaction among processes Consider the following sequence:

1. Process P1 invokes the echo procedure and is interrupted immediately after getchar returns its value and stores it in chin. At this point, the most recently entered character, x, is stored in variable chin.
2. Process P2 is activated and invokes the echo procedure, which runs to conclusion, inputting and then displaying a single character, y, on the screen.
3. Process P1 is resumed. By this time, the value x has been overwritten in chin and therefore lost. Instead, chin contains y, which is transferred to chout and displayed.

Thus, the first character is lost and the second character is displayed twice. Because of shared global variable, chin. If one process updates the global variable and then is interrupted, another process may alter the variable before the first process can use its value. However, if only one process at a time may be in that procedure. Then the foregoing sequence would result in the following:

1. Process P1 invokes the echo procedure and is interrupted immediately after the conclusion of the input function. At this point, the most recently entered character x, is stored in variable chin.
2. Process P2 is activated and invokes the echo procedure. However, because P1 is still inside the echo procedure, although currently suspended, P2 is blocked from entering the procedure. Therefore, P2 is suspended awaiting the availability of the echo procedure.\
3. At some later time, process PI is resumed and completes execution of echo. The proper character, x, is displayed.
4. When PI exits' echo, this removes the block on P2. When P2 is later resumed, the echo procedure is successfully invoked.

Therefore, it is necessary to protect shared global variables. And that the only way to do that is to control the code that accesses the variable.

2.9. Race Condition

A race condition occurs when multiple processes or threads read and write data items so that the final result depends on the order of execution of instructions in the multiple processes.

Suppose that two processes, P1 and P2, share the global variable a. At some point in its execution, P1 updates a to the value 1, and at some point in its execution, P2 updates a to the value 2. Thus, the two tasks are in a race to write variable a. In this example the "loser" of the race (the process that updates last) determines the final value of a. Therefore Operating System Concerns of following things

1. The operating system must be able to keep track of the various processes
2. The operating system must allocate and deallocate various resources for each active process.
3. The operating system must protect the data and physical resources of each process against unintended interference by other processes.
4. The functioning of a process, and the output it produces, must be independent of the speed at which its execution is carried out relative to the speed of other concurrent processes.

Process Interaction can be defined as,

- Processes unaware of each other.
- Processes indirectly aware of each other.
- Processes directly aware of each other.

Concurrent processes come into conflict with each other when they are competing for the use of the same resource.

Two or more processes need to access a resource during the course of their execution. Each process is unaware of the existence of the other processes. There is no exchange of information between the competing processes.

2.10. Requirements for Mutual Exclusion

1. Mutual exclusion must be enforced: Only one process at a time is allowed into its critical section, among all processes that have critical sections for the same resource or shared object.
2. A process that halts in its non-critical section must do so without interfering with other processes.
3. It must not be possible for a process requiring access to a critical section to be delayed indefinitely: no deadlock or starvation.
4. When no process is in a critical section, any process that requests entry to its critical section must be permitted to enter without delay.
5. No assumptions are made about relative process speeds or number of processors.
6. A process remains inside its critical section for a finite time only.

2.11. Mutual Exclusion – Software Support

Software approaches can be implemented for concurrent processes that executes on a single processor or a multiprocessor machine with shared main memory.

2.11.1. Dekker's Algorithm

- Dekker's algorithm is for two processes based solely on software. Each of these processes loop indefinitely, repeatedly entering and re-entering its critical section. A process (P0 & P1) that wishes to execute its critical section first enters the igloo and examines the blackboard. The process number is written on the blackboard, that process leaves the igloo and proceeds to critical section. Otherwise that process will wait for its turn. Process re-enters in the igloo to check the blackboard.

It repeats this exercise until it is allowed to enter its critical section. This procedure is known as busy waiting.

- In formal terms, there is a shared global variable: Var turn : 0 : 1;

```
Process 0
-       ---
-       ---
While turn # 0 do (nothing)
<critical section>;
turn := 1;
-       ---
Process 1
-       ---
-       ---
While turn # 1 do (nothing);
<critical section>;
Turn := 0;
-       ----
```

- The above solution satisfy the property of mutual exclusion. Drawback of the solution are as follows:
    1. Processes must strictly alternate in their use of their critical section.
    2. If one process fails, the other process is permanently blocked.

Drawbacks of software solutions.

1. Complicated to program.
2. Busy waiting is possible.
3. It would be more efficient to block processes that are waiting.
4. Makes difficult assumptions about the memory system.

2.12. Mutual Exclusion – Hardware Support

2.12.1. Interrupt Disabling

In a uniprocessor machine, concurrent processes cannot be overlapped; they can only be interleaved. Furthermore, a process will continue to run until it invokes an operating system service or until it is interrupted. Therefore, to guarantee mutual exclusion, it is sufficient to prevent a process from being interrupted. This capability can be provided in the form of primitives defined by the system kernel for disabling and enabling interrupts.

Eg

```
while (true)
(
disable interrupts()
critical section
enable interrupts()
) remainder
```

Because the critical section cannot be interrupted, mutual exclusion is guaranteed.

Disadvantages

- It works only in a single processor environment.
- Interrupts can be lost if not serviced promptly.
- A process waiting to enter its critical section could suffer from starvation.

2.12.2. Test and Set Instruction

- It is special machine instruction used to avoid mutual exclusion. The test and set instruction can be defined as follows:

```
booleantestset (int i)
{
if (i==o)
{
i=1;
return true;
}
else
{
return false;
}
```

The above function is carried out automatically.

Advantages

1. It is simple and easy to verify.
2. It is applicable to any number of processes.
3. It can b used to support multiple critical section.

Disadvantages

1. Busy waiting is possible.
2. Starvation is also possible.
3. There may be deadlock.

2.13. Semaphores

- The solutions of the critical section problem represented in the section is not easy to generalize to more complex problems. To overcome this difficulty, we can use a synchronization tool call a semaphore. A semaphore S is an integer variable that, a part from initialization, is a accessed two standard atomic operations: wait and signal. This operations were originally termed P.
- The Classical definition of wait and signal are

```
Wait (S)
{
while (S <=0)
S =S – 1;
}
signal(S)
{
S = S + 1;
}
```

- The integer value of the semaphore in the wait and signal operations must be executed indivisibly. That is, when one process modifies the semaphore value, no other process can simultaneously modify that same semaphore value.
- In addition, in the case of the wait(S), the testing of the integer value of S (S0), and its possible modification (S := S – 1), must also be executed without interruption.
- Semaphores are not provided by hardware. But they have several attractive properties:
    1. Semaphores are machine independent.
    2. Semaphores are simple to implement.
    3. Correctness is easy to determine.
    4. Can have many different critical sections with different semaphores.
    5. Semaphore acquire many resources simultaneously.

Drawback of Semaphore

1. They are essentially shared global variables.

2. Access to semaphores can come from anywhere in a program.
3. There is no control or guarantee of proper usage.
4. There is no linguistic connection between the semaphore and the data to which the semaphore controls access.
5. They serve two purposes, mutual exclusion and scheduling constraints.

Readers-Writers Problem

Consider a situation where we have a file shared between many people.

- If one of the people tries editing the file, no other person should be reading or writing at the same time, otherwise changes will not be visible to him/her.
- However, if some person is reading the file, then others may read it at the same time.

Precisely in OS we call this situation as the **readers-writers problem.**

Problem parameters:

- One set of data is shared among a number of processes
- Once a writer is ready, it performs its write. Only one writer may write at a time
- If a process is writing, no other process can read it
- If at least one reader is reading, no other process can write
- Readers may not write and only read

Solution When Reader has the Priority over Writer

Here priority means, no reader should wait if the share is currently opened for reading.

Three variables are used: **mutex, wrt, readcnt** to implement solution

1. **semaphore** mutex, wrt; // semaphore **mutex** is used to ensure mutual exclusion when **readcnt** is updated i.e. when any reader enters or exit from the critical section and semaphore **wrt** is used by both readers and writers
2. **int**readcnt; // **readcnt** tells the number of processes performing read in the critical section, initially 0

Functions for Sempahore

– wait() : decrements the semaphore value.

– signal() : increments the semaphore value.

Writer Process

1. Writer requests the entry to critical section.

2. If allowed i.e. wait() gives a true value, it enters and performs the write. If not allowed, it keeps on waiting.
3. It exits the critical section.

```
do {
    // writer requests for critical section
    wait(wrt);
    // performs the write
    // leaves the critical section
    signal(wrt);
  } while(true);
```

Reader Process

1. Reader requests the entry to critical section.
2. If allowed:
    - It increments the count of number of readers inside the critical section. If this reader is the first reader entering, it locks the **wrt** semaphore to restrict the entry of writers if any reader is inside.
    - It then, signals mutex as any other reader is allowed to enter while others are already reading.
    - After performing reading, it exits the critical section. When exiting, it checks if no more reader is inside, it signals the semaphore "wrt" as now, writer can enter the critical section.
3. If not allowed, it keeps on waiting.

```
do {
  // Reader wants to enter the critical section
  wait(mutex);
  // The number of readers has now increased by 1
  readcnt++;
  // there is atleast one reader in the critical section
  // this ensure no writer can enter if there is even one reader
  // thus we give preference to readers here
  if (readcnt==1)
    wait(wrt);
  // other readers can enter while this current reader is inside
  // the critical section
```

```
signal(mutex);
// current reader performs reading here
wait(mutex);  // a reader wants to leave
readcnt--;
// that is, no reader is left in the critical section,
if (readcnt == 0)
  signal(wrt);      // writers can enter
signal(mutex); // reader leaves
} while(true);
```

Thus, the semaphore '**wrt**' is queued on both readers and writers in a manner such that preference is given to readers if writers are also there. Thus, no reader is waiting simply because a writer has requested to enter the critical section.

Dining Philosophers Problem

The Dining Philosopher Problem – The Dining Philosopher Problem states that K philosophers seated around a circular table with one chopstick between each pair of philosophers. There is one chopstick between each philosopher. A philosopher may eat if he can pickup the two chopsticks adjacent to him. One chopstick may be picked up by any one of its adjacent followers but not both.

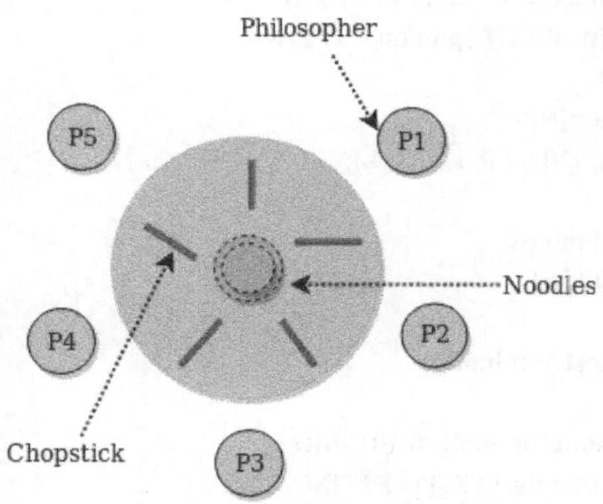

Semaphore Solution to Dining Philosopher

Each philosopher is represented by the following pseudocode:

```
process P[i]
while true do
```

```
{ THINK;
    PICKUP(CHOPSTICK[i], CHOPSTICK[i+1 mod 5]);
    EAT;
    PUTDOWN(CHOPSTICK[i], CHOPSTICK[i+1 mod 5])
  }
```

There are three states of philosopher: **THINKING, HUNGRY and EATING.** Here there are two semaphores: Mutex and a semaphore array for the philosophers. Mutex is used such that no two philosophers may access the pickup or putdown at the same time. The array is used to control the behavior of each philosopher. But, semaphores can result in deadlock due to programming errors.

Code

```
#include <pthread.h>
#include <semaphore.h>
#include <stdio.h>

#define N 5
#define THINKING 2
#define HUNGRY 1
#define EATING 0
#define LEFT (phnum + 4) % N
#define RIGHT (phnum + 1) % N

intstate[N];
intphil[N] = { 0, 1, 2, 3, 4 };

sem_t mutex;
sem_t S[N];

voidtest(intphnum)
{
  if(state[phnum] == HUNGRY
    &&state[LEFT] != EATING
    &&state[RIGHT] != EATING) {
    // state that eating
    state[phnum] = EATING;

    sleep(2);
```

```
        printf("Philosopher %d takes fork %d and %d\n",
                phnum + 1, LEFT + 1, phnum + 1);

        printf("Philosopher %d is Eating\n", phnum + 1);

        // sem_post(&S[phnum]) has no effect
        // during takefork
        // used to wake up hungry philosophers
        // during putfork
        sem_post(&S[phnum]);
    }
}

// take up chopsticks
voidtake_fork(intphnum)
{

    sem_wait(&mutex);

    // state that hungry
    state[phnum] = HUNGRY;

    printf("Philosopher %d is Hungry\n", phnum + 1);

    // eat if neighbours are not eating
    test(phnum);

    sem_post(&mutex);

    // if unable to eat wait to be signalled
    sem_wait(&S[phnum]);

    sleep(1);
}

// put down chopsticks
voidput_fork(intphnum)
{

    sem_wait(&mutex);
```

```
  // state that thinking
  state[phnum] = THINKING;

  printf("Philosopher %d putting fork %d and %d down\n",
      phnum + 1, LEFT + 1, phnum + 1);
  printf("Philosopher %d is thinking\n", phnum + 1);

  test(LEFT);
  test(RIGHT);

  sem_post(&mutex);
}

void* philospher(void* num)
{

  while(1) {

    int* i = num;

    sleep(1);

    take_fork(*i);

    sleep(0);

    put_fork(*i);
  }
}

intmain()
{

  inti;
  pthread_tthread_id[N];

  // initialize the semaphores
  sem_init(&mutex, 0, 1);

  for(i = 0; i< N; i++)
```

```
        sem_init(&S[i], 0, 0);
    for(i = 0; i< N; i++) {

        // create philosopher processes
        pthread_create(&thread_id[i], NULL,
                philospher, &phil[i]);

        printf("Philosopher %d is thinking\n", i + 1);
    }
    for(i
= 0; i< N; i++)

        pthread_join(thread_id[i], NULL);
}
```

2.14. Monitors

- The monitor is a programming-language construct that provides equivalent functionality to that of semaphores and that is easier to control. The monitor construct has been implemented in a number of programming languages, including Concurrent Pascal, Pascal-Plus, Modula-2, Modula-3, and Java. It has also been implemented as a program library. This allows programmers to put monitor locks on any object.
- A monitor supports synchronization by the use of condition variables that are contained Within the monitor and accessible only within the monitor. Condition variables are a special data type in monitors, which are operated on by two functions.
- cwait (c): Suspend execution of the calling process on condition c. The monitor is now available for use by another process.
- csignal (c): Resume execution of some process blocked after a cwait on the same condition)If there are several such processes, choose one of them; if there is no such process, do nothing.
- Monitor wait and signal operations are different from those for the semaphore. If a process in a monitor signals and no task is waiting on the condition variable, the signal is lost.
- Although a process can enter the monitor by invoking any of its procedures, we can think of the monitor as having a single entry point that is guarded so that only one process may be in the monitor at a time. Other processes that attempt to enter the monitor join a queue of processes blocked waiting for monitor availability.

- Once a process is in the monitor, it may temporarily block itself on condition x by issuing cwait (x); it is then placed in a queue of processes waiting to re enter the monitor when the condition changes, and resume execution at the point in its program following the cwait (x) call.
- If a process that is executing in the monitor detects a change in condition variable x, it issues csignal (x), which alerts the corresponding condition queue that the condition has changed.
- A producer can add characters to the buffer only by means of the procedure append inside the monitor; the producer does not have direct access to buffer.
- The procedure first-checks the condition not full to determine if there is space available in the buffer. If not, the process executing the monitor is blocked on that condition.

2.15. Operating System Scheduling Algorithms

CPU Scheduling: Scheduling Criteria

There are many different criterias to check when considering the **"best"** scheduling algorithm, they are:

CPU Utilization

To make out the best use of CPU and not to waste any CPU cycle, CPU would be working most of the time(Ideally 100% of the time). Considering a real system, CPU usage should range from 40% (lightly loaded) to 90% (heavily loaded.)

Throughput

It is the total number of processes completed per unit time or rather say total amount of work done in a unit of time. This may range from 10/second to 1/hour depending on the specific processes.

Turnaround Time

It is the amount of time taken to execute a particular process, i.e. The interval from time of submission of the process to the time of completion of the process(Wall clock time).

Waiting Time

The sum of the periods spent waiting in the ready queue amount of time a process has been waiting in the ready queue to acquire get control on the CPU.

Load Average

It is the average number of processes residing in the ready queue waiting for their turn to get into the CPU.

Response Time

Amount of time it takes from when a request was submitted until the first response is produced. Remember, it is the time till the first response and not the completion of process execution (final response).

In general CPU utilization and Throughput are maximized and other factors are reduced for proper optimization. A Process Scheduler schedules different processes to be assigned to the CPU based on particular scheduling algorithms. There are six popular process scheduling algorithms which we are going to discuss in this chapter –

- First-Come, First-Served (FCFS) Scheduling.
- Shortest-Job-Next (SJN) Scheduling.
- Priority Scheduling.
- Shortest Remaining Time.
- Round Robin (RR) Scheduling.
- Multiple-Level Queues Scheduling.

These algorithms are either **non-preemptive or preemptive**. Non-preemptive algorithms are designed so that once a process enters the running state, it cannot be preempted until it completes its allotted time, whereas the preemptive scheduling is based on priority where a scheduler may preempt a low priority running process anytime when a high priority process enters into a ready state.

First Come First Serve (FCFS)

- Jobs are executed on first come, first serve basis.
- It is a non-preemptive, pre-emptive scheduling algorithm.
- Easy to understand and implement.
- Its implementation is based on FIFO queue.
- Poor in performance as average wait time is high.

Calculating Average Waiting Time

For every scheduling algorithm, **Average waiting time** is a crucial parameter to judge it's performance.

AWT or Average waiting time is the average of the waiting times of the processes in the queue, waiting for the scheduler to pick them for execution.

PROCESS	BURST TIME
P1	21
P2	3
P3	6
P4	2

The average waiting time will be = (0 + 21 + 24 + 30)/4 = 18.75 ms

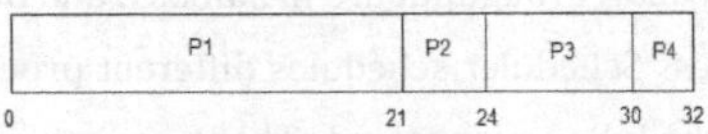

This is the GANTT chart for the above processes

Lower the Average Waiting Time, better the scheduling algorithm.

Consider the processes P1, P2, P3, P4 given in the below table, arrives for execution in the same order, with **Arrival Time** 0, and given **Burst Time**, let's find the average waiting time using the FCFS scheduling algorithm.

The average waiting time will be 18.75 ms.

For the above given proccesses, first **P1** will be provided with the CPU resources,

- Hence, waiting time for **P1** will be 0
- **P1** requires 21 ms for completion, hence waiting time for **P2** will be 21 ms
- Similarly, waiting time for process **P3** will be execution time of **P1** + execution time for **P2**, which will be (21 + 3) ms = 24 ms.
- For process **P4** it will be the sum of execution times of **P1**, **P2** and **P3**.

The **GANTT chart** above perfectly represents the waiting time for each process.

Process	Arrival Time	Execute Time	Service Time
P0	0	5	0
P1	1	3	5
P2	2	8	8
P3	3	6	16

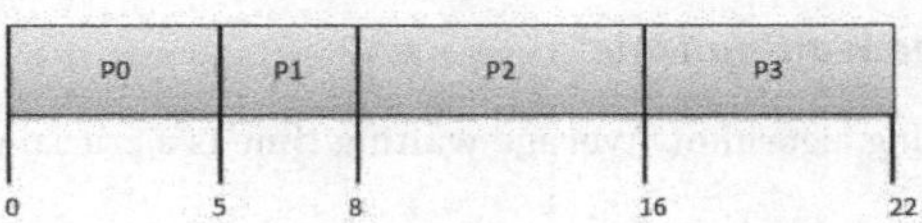

Wait time of each process is as follows.

Process	**Wait Time : Service Time - Arrival Time**
P0	0 - 0 = 0
P1	5 - 1 = 4
P2	8 - 2 = 6
P3	16 - 3 = 13

Average Wait Time: (0+4+6+13) / 4 = 5.75

Shortest Job Next (SJN)

- This is also known as **shortest job first**, or SJF
- This is a non pre-emptive, pre-emptive scheduling algorithm.
- Best approach to minimize waiting time.
- Easy to implement in Batch systems where required CPU time is known in advance.
- Impossible to implement in interactive systems where required CPU time is not known.
- The processer should know in advance how much time process will take.

Process	**Arrival Time**	**Execute Time**	**Service Time**
P0	0	5	3
P1	1	3	0
P2	2	8	14
P3	3	6	8

Gantt Chart

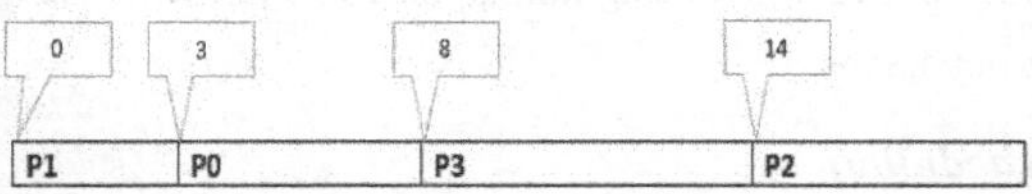

Wait time of each process is as follows.

Process	**Wait Time : Service Time - Arrival Time**
P0	3 - 0 = 3
P1	0
P2	14 - 2 = 12
P3	8 - 3 = 5

Average Wait Time: (3+12+5) / 4 = 5

Consider the below processes available in the ready queue for execution, with **arrival time** as 0 for all and given **burst times.**

PROCESS	BURST TIME
P1	21
P2	3
P3	6
P4	2

In Shortest Job First Scheduling, the shortest Process is executed first.

Hence the GANTT chart will be following :

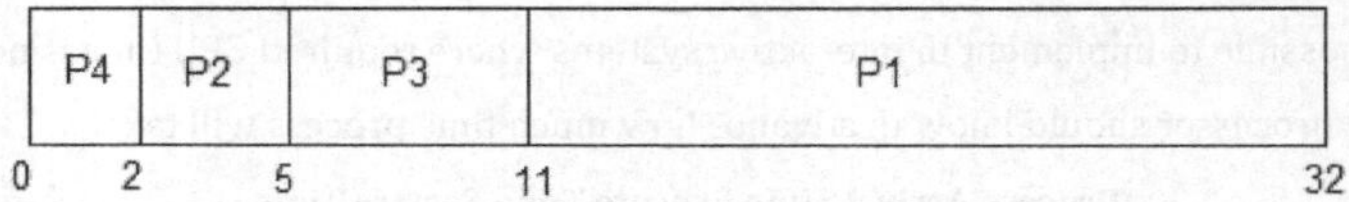

Now, the average waiting time will be = (0 + 2 + 5 + 11)/4 = 4.5 ms

As you can see in the **GANTT chart** above, the process **P4** will be picked up first as it has the shortest burst time, then **P2**, followed by **P3** and at last **P1**.

We scheduled the same set of processes using the First come first serve algorithm in the previous tutorial, and got average waiting time to be 18.75 ms, whereas with SJF, the average waiting time comes out 4.5 ms.

Priority Based Scheduling

- Priority scheduling is a non-preemptive algorithm and one of the most common scheduling algorithms in batch systems.
- Each process is assigned a priority. Process with highest priority is to be executed first and so on.
- Processes with same priority are executed on first come first served basis.
- Priority can be decided based on memory requirements, time requirements or any other resource requirement.

Process	Arrival Time	Execute Time	Priority	Service Time
P0	0	5	1	9
P1	1	3	2	6
P2	2	8	1	14
P3	3	6	3	0

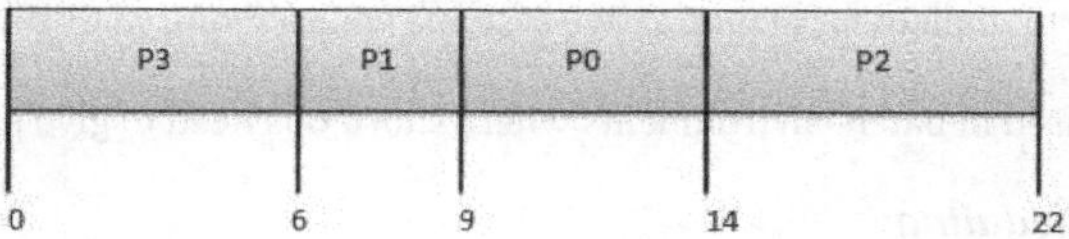

Wait time of each process is as follows.

Process Wait Time : Service Time - Arrival Time

P0	9 - 0 = 9
P1	6 - 1 = 5
P2	14 - 2 = 12
P3	0 - 0 = 0

Average Wait Time: (9+5+12+0) / 4 = 6.5

PROCESS	BURST TIME	PRIORITY
P1	21	2
P2	3	1
P3	6	4
P4	2	3

The GANTT chart for following processes based on Priority scheduling will be,

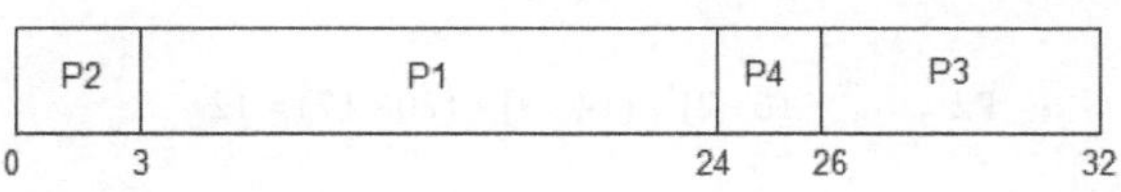

The average waiting time will be, (0 + 3 + 24 + 26)/4 = 13.25 ms

Shortest Remaining Time

- Shortest remaining time (SRT) is the preemptive version of the SJN algorithm.
- The processor is allocated to the job closest to completion but it can be preempted by a newer ready job with shorter time to completion.
- Impossible to implement in interactive systems where required CPU time is not known.
- It is often used in batch environments where short jobs need to give preference.

Round Robin Scheduling

- Round Robin is the preemptive process scheduling algorithm.
- Each process is provided a fix time to execute, it is called a **quantum**.
- Once a process is executed for a given time period, it is preempted and other process executes for a given time period.
- Context switching is used to save states of preempted processes.

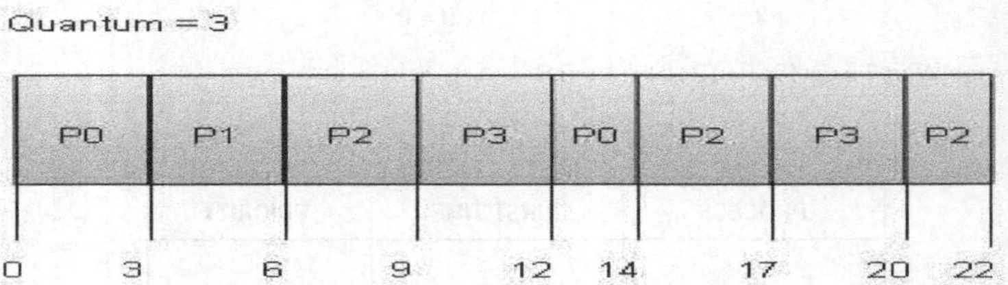

Wait time of each process is as follows.

Process Wait Time : Service Time - Arrival Time

P0	(0 - 0) + (12 - 3) = 9
P1	(3 - 1) = 2
P2	(6 - 2) + (14 - 9) + (20 - 17) = 12
P3	(9 - 3) + (17 - 12) = 11

Average Wait Time: (9+2+12+11) / 4 = 8.5

PROCESS	BURST TIME
P1	21
P2	3
P3	6
P4	2

The GANTT chart for round robin scheduling will be.

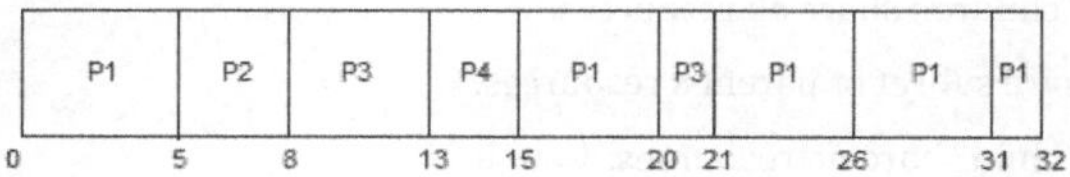

The average waiting time will be, 11 ms.

Multiple-Level Queues Scheduling

Multiple-level queues are not an independent scheduling algorithm. They make use of other existing algorithms to group and schedule jobs with common characteristics.

- Multiple queues are maintained for processes with common characteristics.
- Each queue can have its own scheduling algorithms.
- Priorities are assigned to each queue.

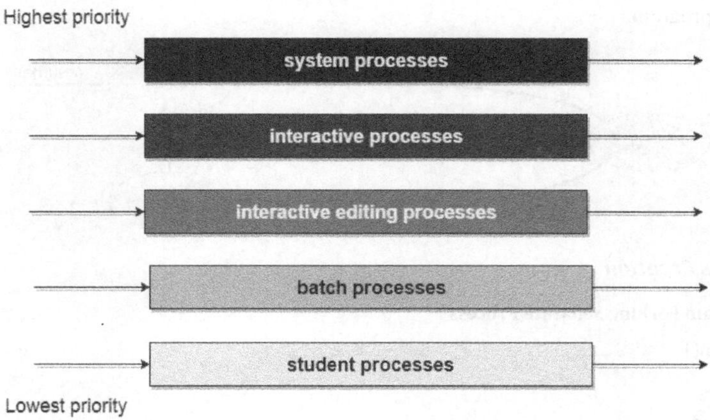

For example, CPU-bound jobs can be scheduled in one queue and all I/O-bound jobs in another queue. The Process Scheduler then alternately selects jobs from each queue and assigns them to the CPU based on the algorithm assigned to the queue.

Process Creation

- Parent process create children processes, which, in turn create other processes, forming a tree of processes.
- Generally, process identified and managed via a process identifier (pid).
- Resource sharing.
- Parent and children share all resources.
- Children share subset of parent's resources.
- Parent and child share no resources.
- Execution.
- Parent and children execute concurrently.
- Parent waits until children terminate.
- Address space.
- Child duplicate of parent.
- Child has a program loaded into it.
- UNIX examples.
- Fork system call creates new process.
- Exec system call used after a fork to replace the process' memory space with a new program.

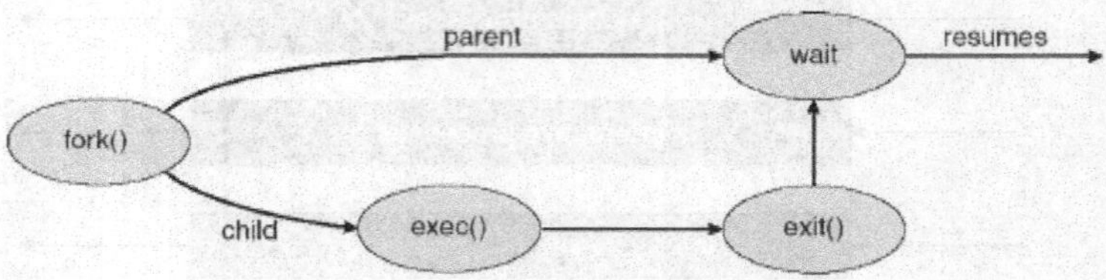

Process Creation

C Program Forking Separate Process

```
int main()
{
pid_t pid;
        /* fork another process */
```

```
        pid = fork();
        if (pid < 0) { /* error occurred */
                fprintf(stderr, "Fork Failed");
                exit(-1);
        }
        else if (pid == 0) { /* child process */
                execlp("/bin/ls", "ls", NULL);
        }
        else { /* parent process */
                /* parent will wait for the child to complete */
                wait (NULL);
                printf ("Child Complete");
                exit(0);
        }
}
```

Process Termination

- Process executes last statement and asks the operating system to delete it (exit).
- Output data from child to parent (via wait).
- Process' resources are deallocated by operating system.
- Parent may terminate execution of children processes (abort).
- Child has exceeded allocated resources.
- Task assigned to child is no longer required.
- If parent is exiting Some operating system do not allow child to continue if its parent terminates.
- All children terminated - cascading termination.

Interprocess Communication

- Processes within a system may be independent or cooperating.
- Cooperating process can affect or be affected by other processes, including sharing data.
- Reasons for cooperating processes:
- Information sharing.
- Computation speedup.
- Modularity.

- Convenience.
- Cooperating processes need interprocess communication (IPC).
- Two models of IPC.
- Shared memory.
- Message passing.

Communications Models

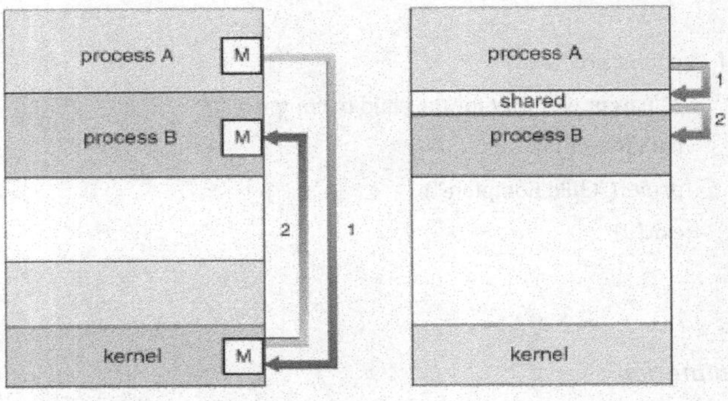

(a) (b)

Producer-Consumer Problem

Paradigm for cooperating processes, *producer* process produces information that is consume d by

consumer process

unbounded-buffer places no practical limit on the size of the buffer

bounded-buffer assumes that there is a fixed buffer size

Bounded-Buffer – Shared-Memory Solution

Shared data

```
#define BUFFER_SIZE 10
typedef struct {
	...
} item;
item buffer[BUFFER_SIZE];
int in = 0;
int out = 0;
```

Solution is correct, but can only use BUFFER_SIZE-1 elements

Bounded-Buffer – Producer

```
        while (true) {
    /* Produce an item */
        while (((in = (in + 1) % BUFFER SIZE count)  == out)
                ;  /* do nothing -- no free buffers */
                buffer[in] = item;
                in = (in + 1) % BUFFER SIZE;
    }
```

Bounded Buffer – Consumer

```
 while (true) {
        while (in == out)
                ; // do nothing -- nothing to consume
                // remove an item from the buffer
                item = buffer[out];
                out = (out + 1) % BUFFER SIZE;
        return item;
    }
```

2.16. Threads

- A thread is a flow of execution through the process code, with its own program counter, system registers and stack. Threads are a popular way to improve application performance through parallelism. A thread is sometimes called a **light weight process.**

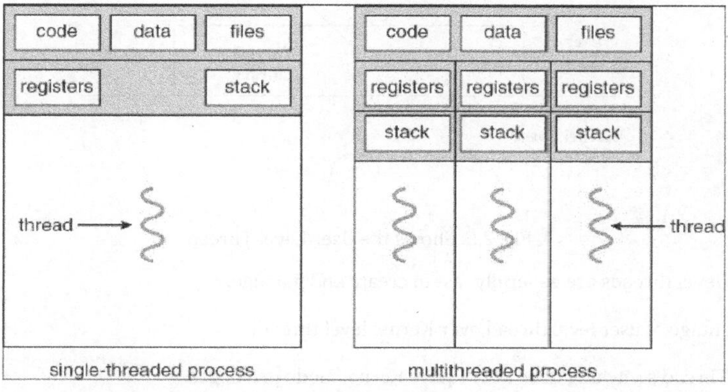

Fig. 2.5: Shows the Single and Multithreaded Process

- Threads represent a software approach to improving performance of operating system by reducing the over head thread is equivalent to a classical process. Each thread belongs to exactly one process and no threadcan exist outside a process. Each thread represents a separate flow of control.
- Threads have been successfully used in implementing network servers. They also provide a suitable foundation for parallel execution of applications on shared memory multiprocessors.

2.17. Types of Thread

Threads is implemented in two ways:

1. User Level
2. Kernel Level

2.17.1. User Level Thread

- In a user thread, all of the work of thread management is done by the application and the kernel is not aware of the existence of threads. The thread library contains code for creating and destroying threads, for passing message and data between threads, for scheduling thread execution and for saving and restoring thread contexts. The application begins with a single thread and begins running in that thread.

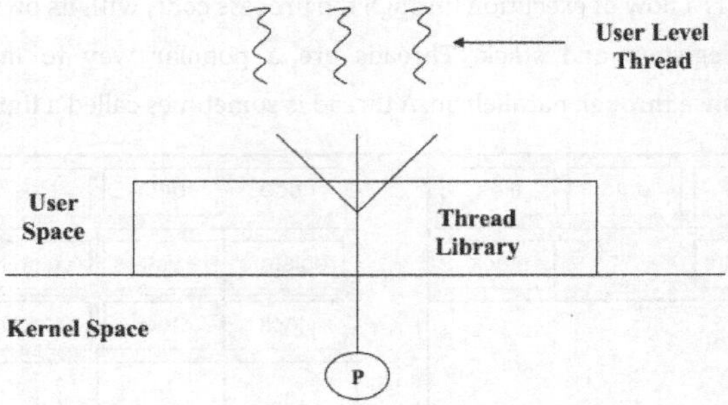

Fig. 2.6: Shows the User Level Thread

User level threads are generally fast to create and manage.

Advantage of user level thread over Kernel level thread:

1. Thread switching does not require Kernel mode privileges.
2. User level thread can run on any operating system.

3. Scheduling can be application specific.
4. User level threads are fast to create and manage.

Disadvantages of user level thread:

1. In a typical operating system, most system calls are blocking.
2. Multithreaded application cannot take advantage of multiprocessing.

2.17.2. Kernel Level Threads

- In Kernel level thread, thread management done by the Kernel. There is no thread management code in the application area. Kernel threads are supported directly by the operating system. Any application can be programmed to be multithreaded. All of the threads within an application are supported within a single process. The Kernel maintains context information for the process as a whole and for individual threads within the process.
- Scheduling by the Kernel is done on a thread basis. The Kernel performs thread creation, scheduling and management in Kernel space. Kernel threads are generally slower to create and manage than the user threads.

Advantages of Kernel Level Thread

1. Kernel can simultaneously schedule multiple threads from the same process on multiple process.
2. If one thread in a process is blocked, the Kernel can schedule another thread of the same process.
3. Kernel routines themselves can multithreaded.

Disadvantages

1. Kernel threads are generally slower to create and manage than the user threads.
2. Transfer of control from one thread to another within same process requires a mode switch to the Kernel.

2.17.3. Advantages of Thread

1. Thread minimize context switching time.
2. Use of threads provides concurrency within a process.
3. Efficient communication.
4. Economy- It is more economical to create and context switch threads.
5. Utilization of multiprocessor architectures.

6. The benefits of multithreading can be greatly increased in a multiprocessor architecture.

2.18. Multithreading Models

- Some operating system provide a combined user level thread and Kernel level thread facility. Solaris is a good example of this combined approach. In a combined system, multiple threads within the same application can run in parallel on multiple processors and a blocking system call need not block the entire process.
- Multithreading models are three types:
  1. Many to many relationship.
  2. Many to one relationship.
  3. One to one relationship.

2.18.1. Many to Many Model

- In this model, many user level threads multiplexes to the Kernel thread of smaller or equal numbers. The number of Kernel threads may be specific to either a particular application or a particular machine.
- Fig. 2.5 shows the many to many model. In this model, developers can create as many user threads as necessary and the corresponding Kernel threads can run in parallels on a multiprocessor.

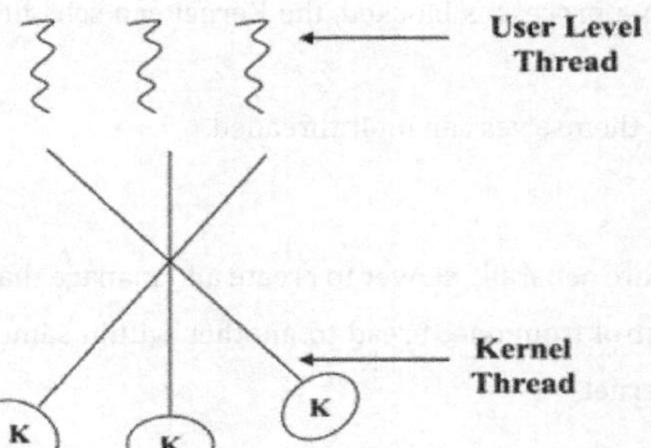

2.18.2. Many to One Model

- Many to one model maps many user level threads to one Kernel level thread. Thread management is done in user space. When thread makes a blocking system call, the entire process will be blocks. Only one thread can access the Kernel at a time, so multiple threads are unable to run in parallel on multiprocessors.

- Fig.2.6 shows the many to one model.

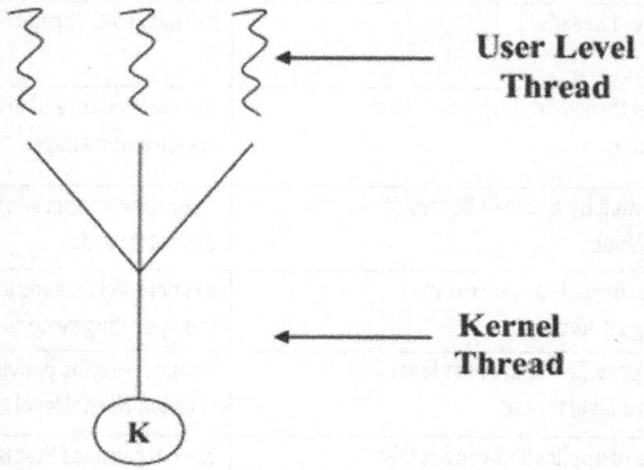

- If the user level thread libraries are implemented in the operating system, that system does not support Kernel threads use the many to one relationship modes.

2.18.3. One to One Model

- There is one to one relationship of user level thread to the kernel level thread. Fig. 2.7 shows one to one relationship model. This model provides more concurrency than the many to one model.

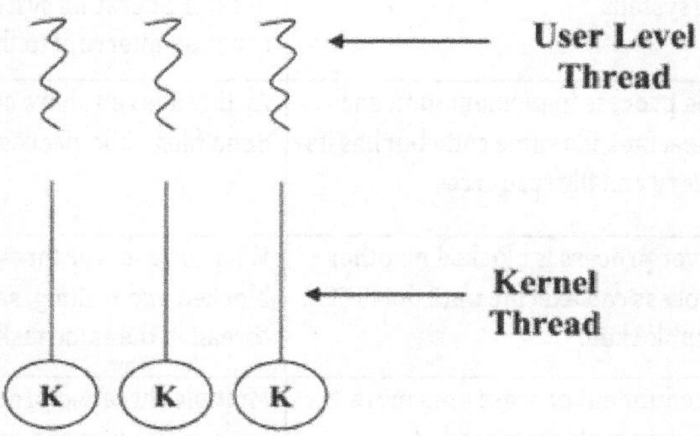

- It also another thread to run when a thread makes a blocking system call. It support multiple thread to execute in parallel on microprocessors. Disadvantage of this model is that creating user thread requires the corresponding Kernel thread. OS/2, windows NT and windows 2000 use one to one relationship model.

2.19. Difference between User Level & Kernel Level Thread

Sr. No	User Level Threads	Kernel Level Thread
1	User level thread are faster to create and manage.	Kernel level thread are slower to create and manage.
2	Implemented by a thread library at the user level.	Operating system support directly to Kernel threads.
3	User level thread can run on any operating system.	Kernel level threads are specific to the operating system.
6	Support provided at the user level called user level thread.	Support may be provided by kernel is called Kernel level threads.
5	Multithread application cannot take advantage of multiprocessing.	Kernel routines themselves can be multithreaded.

2.20. Difference between Process and Thread

Sr. No	Process	Thread
1	Process is called heavy weight process.	Thread is called light weight process.
2	Process switching needs interface with operating system.	Thread switching does not need to call a operating system and cause an interrupt to the Kernel.
3	In multiple process implementation each process executes the same code but has its own memory and file resources.	All threads can share same set of open files, child processes.
6	If one server process is blocked no other server process can execute until the first process unblocked.	While one server thread is blocked and waiting, second thread in the same task could run.
5	Multiple redundant process uses more resources than multiple threaded.	Multiple threaded process uses fewer resources than multiple redundant process.
6	In multiple process each process operates independently of the others.	One thread can read, write or even completely wipe out another threads stack.

2.21. Threading Issues

- System calls fork and exec is discussed here. In a multithreaded programenvironment, fork and exec system calls is changed. Unix system have two version of fork system calls. One call duplicates all threads and another that duplicates only the thread that invoke the fork system call. Whether to use one or two version of fork system call totally depends upon the application. Duplicating all threads is unnecessary, if exec is called immediately after fork system call.
- Thread cancellation is a process of thread terminates before its completion of task. For example, in multiple thread environment, thread concurrently searching through a database. If any one thread returns the result, the remaining thread might be cancelled.
- Thread cancellation is of two types.
  1. Asynchronous cancellation.
  2. Synchronous cancellation.
- In asynchronous cancellation, one thread immediately terminates the target thread. Deferred cancellation periodically check for terminate by target thread. It also allow the target thread to terminate itself in an orderly fashion. Some resources are allocated to the thread. If we cancel the thread, which update the data with other thread. This problem may face by asynchronous cancellation system wide resource are not free if threads cancelled asynchronously. Most of the operating system allow a process or thread to be cancelled asynchronously.

2.22. Summary

A process is a program in execution. As a process executes, it changes state. The state of a process is defined by that process current activity. Each process may be in one of the following states: new, ready, running, waiting, or terminated. Each process is represented in the operating system by its own process control block (PCB).

A process, when it is not executing, placed in some waiting queue. There are two major classes of queues in an operating system: I/O request queues and the ready queue. The ready queue contains all the processes that are ready to execute and are waiting for the CPU. Each process is represented by a PCB and the PCBs can be linked together to form a ready queue. Long-term (job) scheduling is the selection of processes that will be allowed to contend for the CPU. Normally, long- term scheduling is heavily influenced by resources-allocation considerations, especially memory management. Short-term (CPU) scheduling is the selection of one process from the ready queue.

Operating systems must provide a mechanism for parent processes to create new child processes. The parent may wait for its children to terminate before proceeding, or the parent and children may execute concurrently. There are several reasons for allowing concurrent execution: information sharing computation speedup, modularity, and convenience.

The processes executing in the operating system may be either independent processes or cooperating processes. Cooperating processes require an inter-process communication mechanism to communicate with each other. Principally, communication is achieved through two schemes: shared memory and message passing. The shared-memory method requires communicating processes throughthe use of these shared variables. In a shared-memory system, the responsibility for providing communication rests with the application programmers: the operating system needs to provide only the shared memory. The responsibility for providing communication may rest with the operating system itself. These two schemes are not mutually exclusive and can be used simultaneously within a single operating system.

Critical section is a code that only one process at a time can be executing. Critical section problem is design an algorithm that allows at most one process into the critical section at a time, without deadlock. Solution of the critical section problem must satisfy mutual exclusion, progress, bounded waiting.

Semaphore is a synchronization variable that tasks on positive integer values. Binary semaphore are those that have only two values 0 and 1. Semaphores are not provided by hardware. Semaphore is used to solve critical section problem.

A monitor is a software module consisting of one or more procedures, an initialization sequence and local data. Components of monitors are shared data declaration, shared data initialization, operations on shared data and synchronization statement.

A thread is a flow of control within a process. A multithreaded process contains several different flows of control within the same address space. The benefits of multithreading include increased responsiveness to the user, resource sharing within the process, economy, and scalability issues such as more efficient use of multiple core.

User level threads are threads are visible to the programmer and are unknown to the kernel. The operating system kernel supports and manages kernel level threads. In general, user level threads are faster to create and manage than are kernel threads, as no intervention from the kernel is required. Three different types of models relate user and kernel threads: the many-to-one model maps many user threads to a single thread.

The one to one model maps each user thread to a corresponding kernel thread. The many to many model multiplexers many user threads to a smaller or equal number of kernel threads.

2.23. Model Questions

Q.1 Define process and programs?

Q.2 Describe Process Control Block?

Q.3 Explain Scheduling Queues?

Q.4 Explain schedulers and its types?

Q.5 Differentiate various types of scheduler?

Q.6 Explain context switch?

Q.7 Explain operation on processes?

Q.8 Explain in brief race condition?

Q.9 Define the term critical section?

Q.10 What are the requirement for critical section problem?

Q.11 Write a short note on:

a) Semaphore

b) Monitors

Q.12 What are semaphores? How do they implement mutual exclusion?

Q.13 Describe hardware solution to the critical section problem?

Q.14 Define thread and its types in detail?

Q.15 Differentiate user level thread and kernel level thread?

Q.16 Explain various Multithreaded Model?

Q.17 Differentiate process and thread?

2.24. Objective Questions

1. The number of processes completed per unit time is known as ________

   a) Output

   b) Throughput

   c) Efficiency

   d) Capacity

2. A Process Control Block (PCB) does not contain which of the following:

a) Code

b) Stack

c) Bootstrap program

d) Data

3. The Process Control Block is,

a) Process type variable

b) Data Structure

c) A secondary storage section

d) A Block in memory

4. The degree of multiprogramming is,

a) The number of processes executed per unit time

b) The number of processes in the ready queue

c) The number of processes in the I/O queue

d) The number of processes in memory

5. The entry of all the PCBs of the current processes is in,

a) Process Register

b) Program Counter

c) Process Table

d) Process Unit

6. The objective of multiprogramming is to,

a) Have some process running at all times

b) Have multiple programs waiting in a queue ready to run

c) To minimize CPU utilization

d) None of the mentioned

7. The state of a process is defined by,

a) The final activity of the process

b) The activity just executed by the process

c) The activity to next be executed by the process

d) The current activity of the process

8. Which of the following is not the state of a process?

a) New

b) Old

c) Waiting

d) Running

9. A single thread of control allows the process to perform.

   a) Only one task at a time

   b) Multiple tasks at a time

   c) Only two tasks at a time

   c) All of the mentioned

10. To enforce .... two functions are provided enter-critical and exit-critical, where each function takes as an argument the name of the resource that is the subject of competition.

    a) Mutual Exclusion

    b) Synchronization

    c) Deadlock

    d) Starvation

11. Which of the following facility or capacity are required to provide support for mutual exclusion.

    i) A process that halts in its noncritical section must do so without interfering with other processes.

    ii) Assumption should made about relative process speeds or number of processors.

    iii) A process remains inside its critical section for a finite time only.

    a) i and ii only

    b) ii and iii only

    c) i and iii only

    d) All i, ii and iii

12. .... when a process leaves a critical section and more than one process is waiting, the selection of a waiting process is arbitrary.

    A) Busy waiting is employed

    B) Starvation is possible

    C) Deadlock is possible

    D) All of the above

13. For semaphores and binary semaphores, a .... is used to hold processes waiting on the semaphore.

    A) Stack

    B) Queue

    C) Tree

    D) Graph

14. In .... messages are not send directly from sender to receiver but rather are sent to a shared data structure consisting queues that can temporarily hold messages.

A) Direct addressing

B) Indirect addressing

C) One-to-one-addressing

D) One-to-many addressing

15. .... are useful for the enforcement of mutual exclusion and also provide an effective means of inter-process communication.

A) Semaphores

B) Messages

C) Monitors

D) Addressing

16. A .... is a software module consisting of one or more procedures, an initialization sequence, and local data.

A) Monitor

B) Message passing

C) Strong semaphore

D) Binary semaphore

17. Semaphores provide a primitive yet powerful and flexible tool for enforcing mutual exclusion and for co-coordinating processes called ....

A) Monitor

B) Message passing

C) Strong semaphore

D) Binary semaphore

18. For semaphores and binary semaphores, a .... is used to hold processes waiting on the semaphore.

A) Stack

B) Queue

C) Tree

D) Graph

19. .... techniques can be use to resolve conflicts, such as competition for resources, and synchronize processes so that they can co-operate.

A) Mutual Exclusion

B) Synchronization

C) Deadlock

D) Starvation

20. __________ is used to terminate the process. **(Delete)**

21. The ___________ contains all the processes that are ready to execute and are waiting for the CPU **(ready queue)**

22. __________ is defined as the current activity of the process. **(Process state)**

23. ______________ is called as CPU scheduler. **(Short- term scheduler)**

24. ____________________is a process that can affect or be affected by the other processes while executing. **(Co-operating process)**

25. Which one of the following is not shared by threads?

a) Program counter

b) Stack

c) Both program counter and stack

d) None of the mentioned

26. If one thread opens a file with read privileges then,

a) Other threads in the other process can also read from that file

b) Other threads in the same process can also read from that file

c) Any other thread can't read from that file

d) All of the mentioned

27. When the event for which a thread is blocked occurs.

a) Thread moves to the ready queue

b) Thread remains blocked

c) Thread completes

d) A new thread is provided

28. Termination of the process terminates.

a) First thread of the process

b) First two threads of the process

c) All threads within the process

d) No thread within the process

29. The register context and stacks of a thread are deallocated when the thread

    a) Terminates

    b) Blocks

    c) Unblocks

    d) Spawns

30. Thread synchronization is required because,

    a) All threads of a process share the same address space

    b) All threads of a process share the same global variables

    c) All threads of a process can share the same files

    d) All of the mentioned

31. Which one of the following is not a valid state of a thread?

    a) Running

    b) Parsing

    c) Ready

    d) Blocked

32. The jacketing technique is used to,

    a) Convert a blocking system call into non-blocking system call

    b) Create a new thread

    c) Communicate between threads

    d) Terminate a thread

33. The time required to create a new thread in an existing process is,

    a) Greater than the time required to create a new process

    b) Less than the time required to create a new process

    c) Equal to the time required to create a new process

    d) None of the mentioned

34. A process can be,

    a) Single threaded

    b) Multithreaded

    c) Both single threaded and multithreaded

    d) None of the mentioned

CHAPTER 3

MEMORY MANAGEMENT IN OS

3.1. Objectives

- To provide a detailed description of various ways of organizing memory hardware.
- To discuss various memory-management techniques, including paging and segmentation.
- To provide a detailed description of the Intel Pentium, which supports both pure segmentation and segmentation with paging.
- To describe the benefits of a virtual memory system.
- To explain the concepts of demand paging, page-replacement algorithms, and allocation of page frames.
- To discuss the principle of the working-set model.

3.2. Memory Management

Memory is central to the operation of a modern computer system. Memory is a large array of words or bytes, each with its own address.

A program resides on a disk as a binary executable file. The program must be brought into memory and placed within a process for it to be executed depending on the memory management in use the process may be moved between disk and memory during its execution. The collection of processes on the disk that are waiting to be brought into memory for execution forms the input queue. i.e. selected one of the process in the input queue and to load that process into memory.

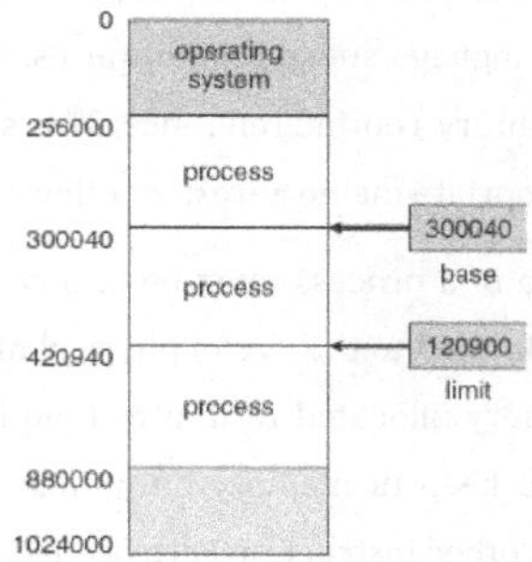

Fig. 3.1: A base and Limit Register Define a Logical Address Space

We can provide protection by using two registers, usually a base and a limit, as shown in fig. 3.1 the base register holds the smallest legal physical memory address; the limit register specifies the size of the range. For example, if the base register holds 300040 and the limit register is 120900, then the program can legally access all addresses from 300040 through 420939(inclusive).

The binding of instructions and data to memory addresses can be done at any step along the way:

- Compile time: If it is known at compile time where the process will reside in memory, then absolute code can be generated.
- Load time: If it is not known at compile time where the process will reside in memory, then the compiler must generate re-locatable code.
- Execution time: If the process can be moved during its execution from one memory segment to another, then binding must be delayed until run time.

3.2.1. Dynamic Loading

Better memory-space utilization can be done by dynamic loading. With dynamic loading, a routine is not loaded until it is called. All routines are kept on disk in a re-locatable load format. The main program is loaded into memory and is executed.

The advantage of dynamic loading is that an unused routine is never loaded.

3.2.2. Dynamic Linking

Most operating systems support only static linking, in which system language libraries are treated like any other object module and are combined by the loader into the binary program image. The concept of dynamic linking is similar to that of dynamic loading. Rather than loading being postponed until execution time, linking is postponed. This feature is usually used with system libraries, such as language subroutine libraries. With dynamic linking, a stub is included in the image for each library-routine reference. This stub is a small piece of code that indicates how to locate the appropriate memory-resident library routing.

The entire program and data of a process must be in physical memory for the process to execute. The size of a process is limited to the size of physical memory. So that a process can be larger than the amount of memory allocated to it, a technique called overlays is sometimes used. The idea of overlays is to keep in memory only those instructions and data that are needed at any given time. When other instructions are needed, they are loaded into space that was occupied previously by instructions that are no longer needed.

Example, consider a two-pass assembler. During pass 1, it constructs a symbol table; then, during pass 2, it generates machine-language code. We may be able to partition such an assembler into pass 1 code, pass 2 code, the symbol table 1, and common support routines used by both pass 1 and pass 2.

Let us consider,

Pass1	70K
Pass2	80K
Symbol table	20K
Common routines	30K

To load everything at once, we would require 200K of memory. If only 150K is available, we cannot run our process. But pass 1 and pass 2 do not need to be in memory at the same time. We thus define two overlays: Overlay A is the symbol table, common routines, and pass 1, and overlay B is the symbol table, common routines, and pass 2. We add an overlay driver (10K) and start with overlay A in memory. When we finish pass 1, we jump to the overlay driver, which reads overlay B into memory, overwriting overlay A, and then transfers control to pass 2. Overlay A needs only 120K, whereas overlay B needs 130K. As in dynamic loading, overlays do not require any special support from the operating system.

3.2.3. Logical versus Physical Address Space

An address generated by the CPU is commonly referred to as a logical address, whereas an address seen by the memory unit is commonly referred to as a physical address. The compile-time and load-time address-binding schemes result in an environment where the logical and physical addresses are the same. The execution- time address-binding scheme results in an environment where the logical and physical addresses differ. In this case, we usually refer to the logical address as a virtual address. The set of all logical addresses generated by a program is referred to as a logical address space; the set of all physical addresses corresponding to these logical addresses is referred to as a physical address space. The run-time mapping from virtual to physical addresses is done by the memory management unit (MMU), which is a hardware device. The base register is called a relocation register.

The value in the relocation register is added to every address generated by a user process at the time it is sent to memory. For example, if the base is at 13000, then an attempt by the user to address location 0 dynamically relocated to location 14,000; an access to location 347 is mapped to location 13347.

The MS-DOS operating system running on the Intel 80x86 family of processors uses four relocation registers when loading and running processes. The user program never sees the real physical addresses. The program can create a pointer to location 347 store it memory, manipulate it, compare it to other addresses all as the number 347. The user program deals with logical addresses. The memory-mapping hardware converts logical addresses into physical addressed Logical addresses (in the range 0 to max) and physical addresses (in the range R + 0 to R + max for a base value R). The user generates only logical addresses. The concept of a logical address space that is bound to a separate physical address space is central to proper memory management.

3.3. Swapping

A process, can be swapped temporarily out of memory to a backing store, and then brought back into memory for continued execution. Assume a multiprogramming environment with a round robin CPU-scheduling algorithm. When a quantum expires, the memory manager will start to swap out the process that just finished, and to swap in another process to the memory space that has been freed (Fig 3.2). When each process finishes its quantum, it will be swapped with another process.

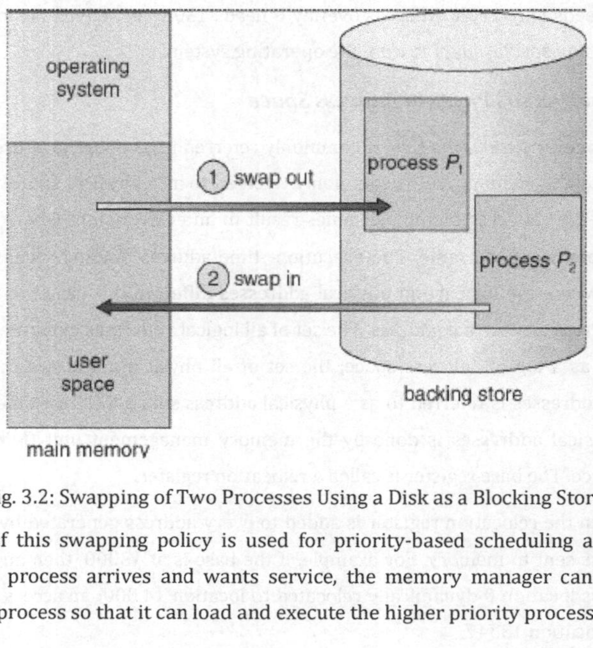

Fig. 3.2: Swapping of Two Processes Using a Disk as a Blocking Store

A variant of this swapping policy is used for priority-based scheduling algorithms. If a higher-priority process arrives and wants service, the memory manager can swap out the lower-priority process so that it can load and execute the higher priority process.

When the higher priority process finishes, the lower-priority process can be swapped back in and continued. This variant of swapping is sometimes called rollout, roll in. A process is swapped out will be swapped back into the same memory space that it occupies previously. If binding is done at assembly or load time, then the process cannot be moved to different location. If execution-time binding is being used, then it is possible to swap a process into a different memory space. Swapping requires a backing store. The backing store is commonly a fast disk. It is large enough to accommodate copies of all memory images for all users. The system maintains a ready queue consisting of all processes whose memory images are on the backing store or in memory and are ready to run.

The context-switch time in such a swapping system is fairly high. Let us assume that the user process is of size 100K and the backing store is a standard hard disk with transfer rate of 1 megabyte per second. The actual transfer of the 100K process to or from memory takes.

$$100K / 1000K \text{ per second} = 1/10 \text{ second}$$
$$= 100 \text{ milliseconds}$$

3.4. Contiguous Allocation

Contiguous Allocation of Disk Space

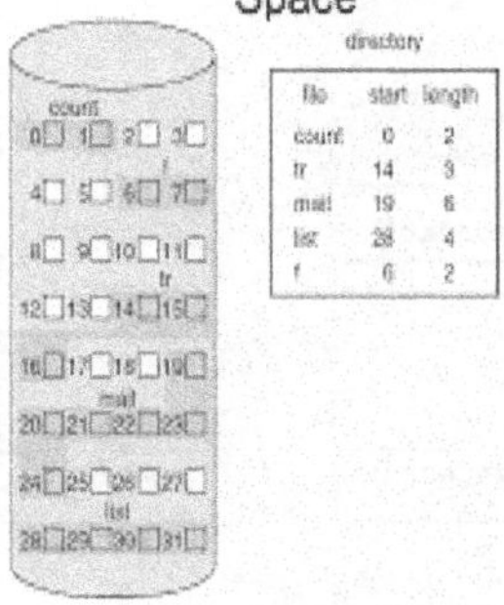

The main memory must accommodate both the operating system and the various user processes. The memory is usually divided into two partitions, one for the resident operating system, and one for the user processes. To place the operating system in low memory. Thus, we shall discuss only me situation where the operating system resides in low memory. The development of the other situation is similar. Common Operating System is placed in low memory.

3.4.1. Single-Partition Allocation

If the operating system is residing in low memory, and the user processes are executing in high memory. And operating-system code and data are protected from changes by the user processes. We also need protect the user processes from one another. We can provide this 2 protection by using a relocation registers. The relocation register contains the value of the smallest physical address; the limit register contains the range of logical addresses (for example, relocation = 100,040 and limit = 74,600). With relocation and limit registers, each logical address must be less than the limit register; the MMU maps the logical address dynamically by adding the value in the relocation register. This mapped address is sent to memory. The relocation-register scheme provides an effective way to allow the operating system size to change dynamically.

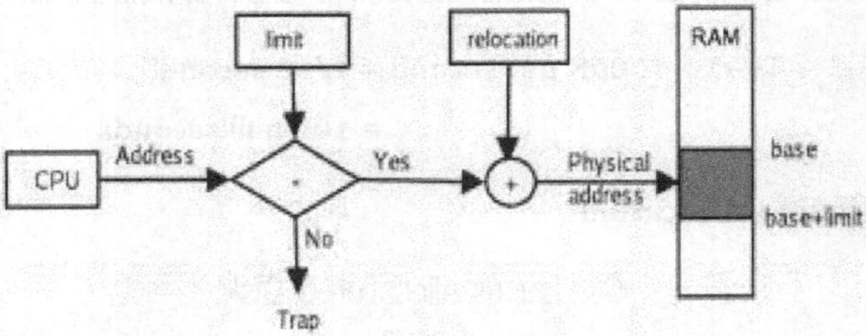

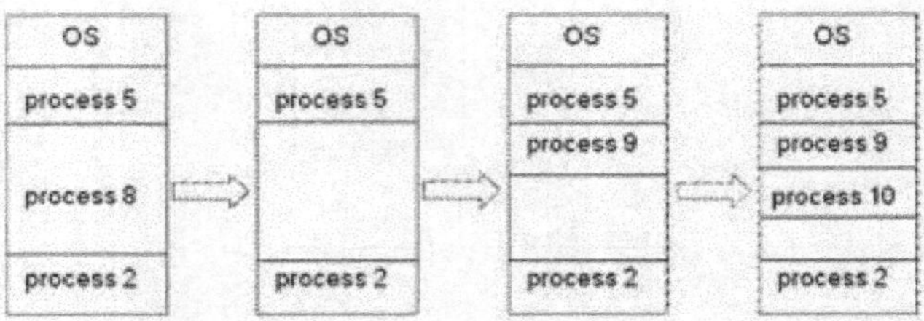

3.4.2. Multiple-Partition Allocation

One of the simplest schemes for memory allocation is to divide memory into a number of fixed-sized partitions. Each partition may contain exactly one process. Thus, the degree of multiprogramming is bound by the number of partitions. When a partition is free, a process is selected from the input queue and is loaded into the free partition. When the process terminates, the partition becomes available for another process. The operating system keeps a table indicating which parts of memory are available and which are occupied.

Initially, all memory is available for user processes, and is considered as one large block, of available memory, a hole. When a process arrives and needs memory, we search for a hole large enough for this process.

For example, assume that we have 2560K of memory available and a resident operating system of 400K. This situation leaves 2160K for user processes. FCFS job scheduling, we can immediately allocate memory to processes P1, P2, P3. Holes size 260K that cannot be used by any of the remaining processes in the input queue. Using a round-robin CPU-scheduling with a quantum of 1 time unit, process will terminate at time 14, releasing its memory. Memory allocation is done using Round-Robin Sequence as shown in fig. When a process arrives and needs memory, we search this set for a hole that is large enough for this process. If the hole is too large, it is split into two: One part is allocated to the arriving process; the other is returned to the set of holes. When a process terminates, it releases its block of memory, which is then placed back in the set of holes. If the new hole is adjacent to other holes, we merge these adjacent holes to form one larger hole.

This procedure is a particular instance of the general dynamic storage-allocation problem, which is how to satisfy a request of size n from a list of free holes. There are many solutions to this problem. The set of holes is searched to determine which hole is best to allocate, first-fit, best-fit, and worst-fit are the most common strategies used to select a free hole from the set of available holes.

- **First-fit:** Allocate the first hole that is big enough. Searching can start either at the beginning of the set of holes or where the previous first-fit search ended. We can stop searching as soon as we find a free hole that is large enough.
- **Best-fit:** Allocate the smallest hole that is big enough. We must search the entire list, unless the list is kept ordered by size. This strategy-produces the smallest leftover hole.
- **Worst-fit:** Allocate the largest hole. Again, we must search the entire list unless it is sorted by size. This strategy produces the largest leftover hole which may be more useful than the smaller leftover hole from a best approach.

3.4.3. External and Internal Fragmentation

As processes are loaded and removed from memory, the free memory space is broken into little pieces. External fragmentation exists when enough to the memory space exists to satisfy a request, but it is not contiguous; storage is fragmented into a large number of small holes. Depending on the total amount of memory storage and the average process size, external fragmentation may be either a minor or a major problem.

Given N allocated blocks, another 0.5N blocks will be lost due to fragmentation. That is, one-third of memory may be unusable. This property is known as the 50- percent rule.

3.5. Paging

External fragmentation is avoided by using paging. In this physical memory is broken into blocks of the same size called pages. When a process is to be executed, its pages are loaded into any available memory frames. Every address generated by the CPU is divided into any two parts: a page number(p) and a page offset(d) (Fig 3.3). The page number is used as an index into a page table. The page table contains the base address of each page in physical memory. This base address is combined with the gage offset to define the physical memory address that is sent to the memory unit.

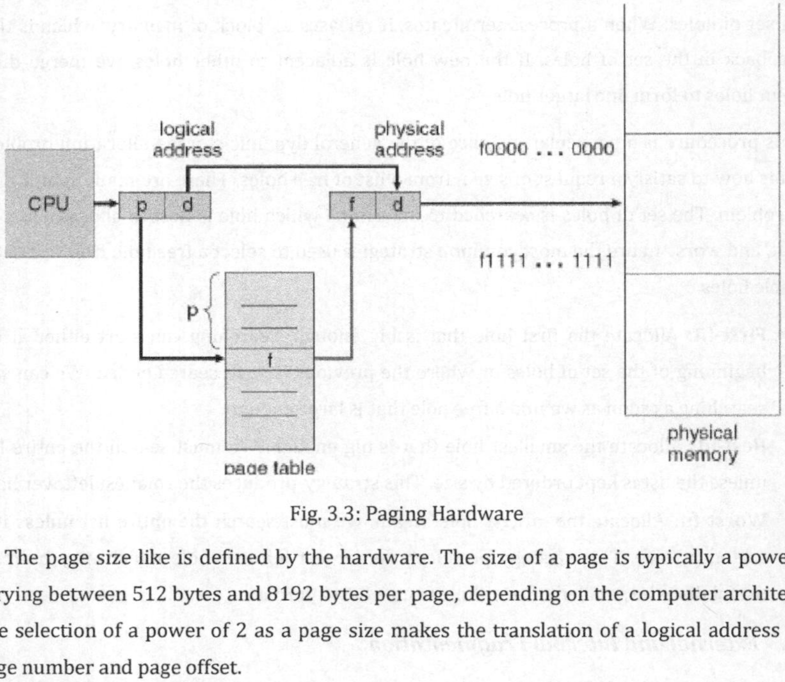

Fig. 3.3: Paging Hardware

The page size like is defined by the hardware. The size of a page is typically a power of 2 varying between 512 bytes and 8192 bytes per page, depending on the computer architecture. The selection of a power of 2 as a page size makes the translation of a logical address into a page number and page offset.

If the size of logical address space is 2m, and a page size is 2n addressing units (bytes or words), then the high-order m - n bits of a logical address designate the page number, and the n low-order bits designate the page offset. Thus, the logical address is as follows:

page number

page offset

p d

m – n n

Where p is an index into the page table and d is the displacement within the page.

Paging is a form of dynamic relocation. Every logical address is bound by the paging hardware to some physical address. When we use a paging scheme, we have no external fragmentation: Any free frame can be allocated to a process that needs it. If process size is independent of page size, we can have internal fragmentation to average one-half page per process. When a process arrives in the system to be executed, its size, expressed in pages, is examined. Each page of the process needs one frame. Thus, if the process requires n pages, there must be at least n frames available in memory. If there are n frames available, they are allocated to this arriving process. The first page of the process is loaded into one of the allocated frames and the frame number is put in the page table for this process. The next page is loaded into another frame, and its frame number is put into the page table, and so on. The user program views that memory as one single contiguous space, containing only this one program. But the user program is scattered throughout physical memory and logical addresses are translated into physical addresses. The operating system is managing physical memory, it must be aware of the allocation details of physical memory: which frames are allocated, which frames are available, how many total frames there are, and so on. This information is generally kept in a data structure called a frame table. The frame table has one entry for each physical page frame, indicating whether the latter is free allocatedand, if it is allocated, to which page of which process or processes. The operating system maintains a copy of the page table for each process. Paging therefore increases the context-switch time.

3.6. Segmentation

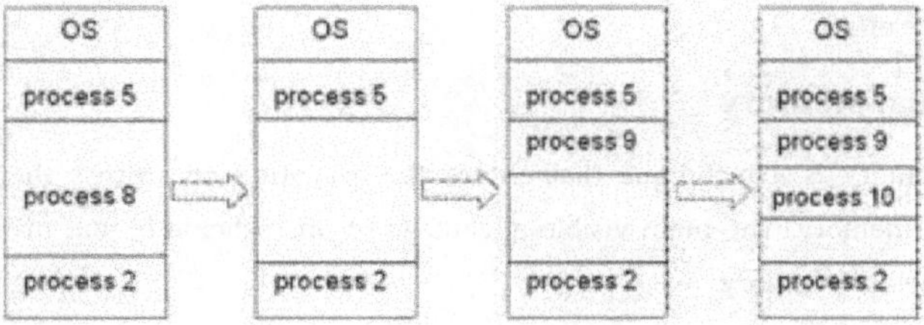

A user program can be subdivided using segmentation, in which the program and its associated data are divided into a number of segments. It is not required that all segments of all programs be of the same length, although there is a maximum segment length. As with paging, a logical address using segmentation consists of two parts, in this case a segment number and an offset. Because of the use of unequal-size segments, segmentation is similar to dynamic partitioning. In segmentation, a program may occupy more than one partition, and these partitions need not be contiguous. Segmentation eliminates internal fragmentation but, like dynamic partitioning, it suffers from external fragmentation. However, because a process is broken up into a number of smaller pieces, the external fragmentation should be less. Whereas paging is invisible to the programmer, segmentation usually visible and is provided as a convenience for organizing programs and data. Another consequence of unequal-size segments is that there is no simple relationship between logical addresses and physical addresses. Segmentation scheme would make use of a segment table for each process and a list of free blocks of main memory.

Each segment table entry would have to as in paging give the starting address in main memory of the corresponding segment. The entry should also provide the length of the segment, to assure that invalid addresses are not used. When a process enters the Running state, the address of its segment table is loaded into a special register used by the memory management hardware. Consider an address of n + m bits, where the leftmost n bits are the segment number and the rightmost m bits are the offset. The following steps are needed for address translation:

- Extract the segment number as the leftmost n bits of the logical address.
- Use the segment number as an index into the process segment table to find the starting physical address of the segment.
- Compare the offset, expressed in the rightmost m bits, to the length of the segment. If the offset is greater than or equal to the length, the address is invalid.
- The desired physical address is the sum of the starting physical address of the segment plus the offset.

3.7. Virtual Memory

Virtual memory is a technique that allows the execution of process that may not be completely in memory. The main visible advantage of this scheme is that programs can be larger than physical memory.

Virtual memory is the separation of user logical memory from physical memory this separation allows an extremely large virtual memory to be provided for programmers when only a smaller physical memory is available (Fig 3.4).

Following are the situations, when entire program is not required to load fully.

1. User written error handling routines are used only when an error occurs in the data or computation.
2. Certain options and features of a program may be used rarely.
3. Many tables are assigned a fixed amount of address space even though only a small amount of the table is actually used.

The ability to execute a program that is only partially in memory would counter many benefits.

1. Less number of I/O would be needed to load or swap each user program into memory.
2. A program would no longer be constrained by the amount of physical memory that is available.
3. Each user program could take less physical memory, more programs could be run the same time, with a corresponding increase in CPU utilization and throughput.

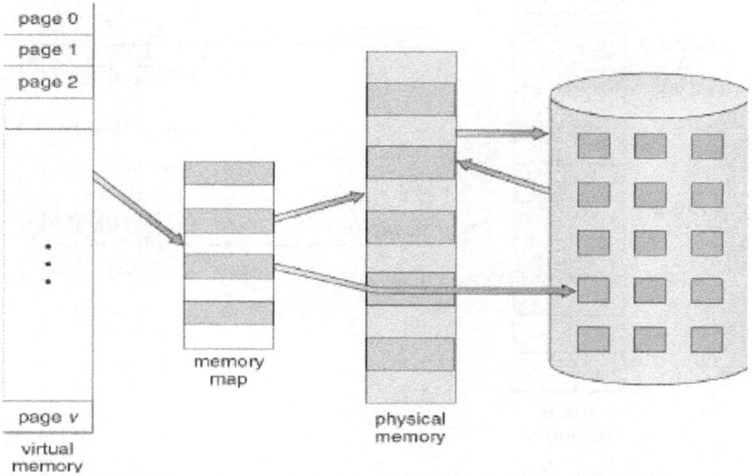

Fig. 3.4: Diagram Showing Virtual Memory that is Larger than Physical Memory

Virtual memory is commonly implemented by demand paging. It can also be implemented in a segmentation system. Demand segmentation can also be used to provide virtual memory.

3.8. Demand Paging

A demand paging is similar to a paging system with swapping(Fig 8.2). When we want to execute a process, we swap it into memory. Rather than swapping the entire process into memory.

When a process is to be swapped in, the pager guesses which pages will be used before the process is swapped out again Instead of swapping in a whole process, the pager brings only those necessary pages into memory. Thus, it avoids reading into memory pages that will not be used in anyway, decreasing the swap time and the amount of physical memory needed.

Hardware support is required to distinguish between those pages that are in memory and those pages that are on the disk using the valid-invalid bit scheme. Where valid and invalid pages can be checked checking the bit and marking a page will have no effect if the process never attempts to access the pages. While the process executes and accesses pages that are memory resident, execution proceeds normally.

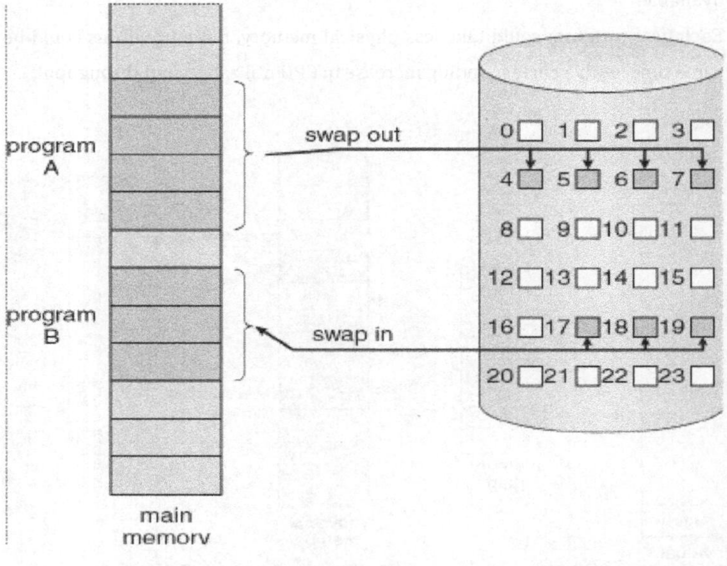

Fig. 3.5: Transfer of a Paged Memory to Continuous Disk Space

Access to a page marked invalid causes a page-fault trap. This trap is the result of the operating system's failure to bring the desired page into memory. But page fault can be handled as following (Fig 3.6):

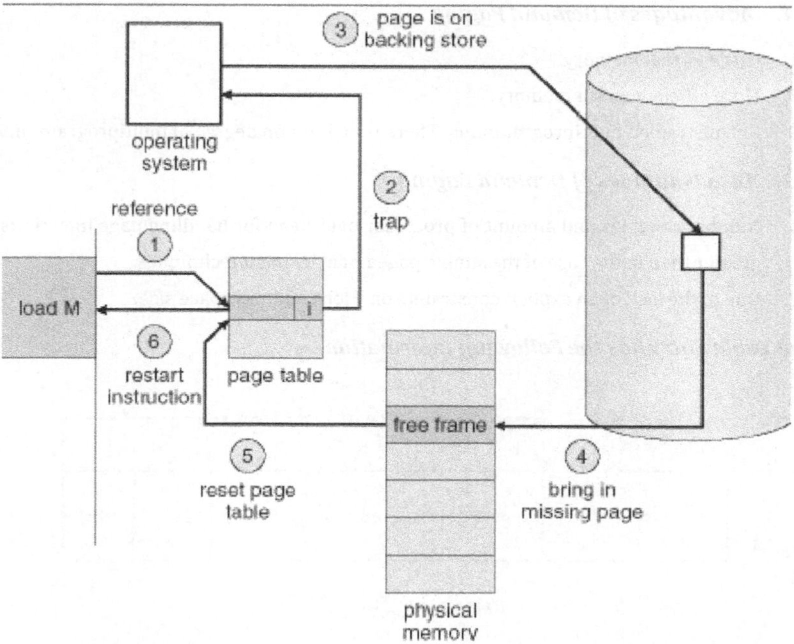

Fig. 3.6: Steps in Handling a Page Fault

1. We check an internal table for this process to determine whether the reference was a valid or invalid memory access.
2. If the reference was invalid, we terminate the process. If .it was valid, but we have not yet brought in that page, we now page in the latter.
3. We find a free frame.
4. We schedule a disk operation to read the desired page into the newly allocated frame.
5. When the disk read is complete, we modify the internal table kept with the process and the page table to indicate that the page is now in memory.
6. We restart the instruction that was interrupted by the illegal address trap. The process can now access the page as though it had always been memory.

Therefore, the operating system reads the desired page into memory and restarts the process as though the page had always been in memory.

The page replacement is used to make the frame free if they are not in used. If no frame is free then other process is called in.

3.8.1. *Advantages of Demand Paging*

1. Large virtual memory.
2. More efficient use of memory.
3. Unconstrained multiprogramming. There is no limit on degree of multiprogramming.

3.8.2. *Disadvantages of Demand Paging*

1. Number of tables and amount of processor over head for handling page interrupts are greater than in the case of the simple paged management techniques.
2. Due to the lack of an explicit constraints on a jobs address space size.

Page Table Entry has the Following Information

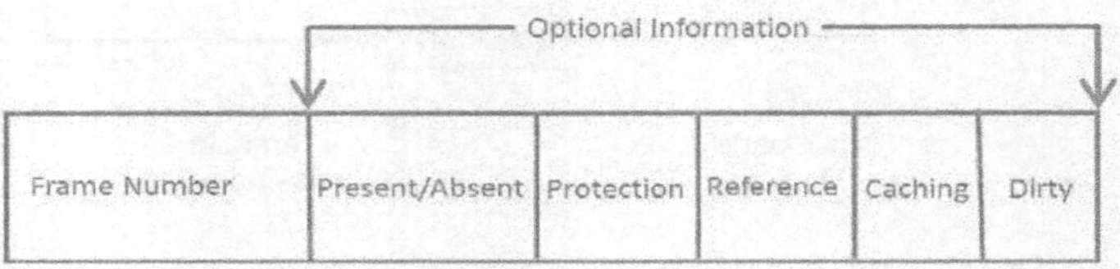

PAGE TABLE ENTRY

1. **Frame Number** – It gives the frame number in which the current page you are looking for is present. The number of bits required depends on the number of frames.
2. Number of bits for frame = Size of physical memory/frame size
3. **Present/Absent bit** – Present or absent bit says whether a particular page you are looking for is present or absent. In case if it is not present, that is called Page Fault. It is set to 0 if the corresponding page is not in memory. Used to control page fault by the operating system to support virtual memory. Sometimes this bit is also known as **valid/invalid** bits.
4. **Protection bit** – Protection bit says that what kind of protection you want on that page. So, these bit for the protection of the page frame (read, write etc).
5. **Referenced bit** – Referenced bit will say whether this page has been referred in the last clock cycle or not. It is set to 1 by hardware when the page is accessed.
6. **Caching enabled/disabled** –Some times we need the fresh data. Let us say the user is typing some information from the keyboard and your program should run according to the input given by the user. In that case, the information will come into the main memory.

Therefore main memory contains the latest information which is typed by the user. Now if you try to put that page in the cache, that cache will show the old information. So whenever freshness is required, we don't want to go for caching or many levels of the memory. The information present in the closest level to the CPU and the information present in the closest level to the user might be different. So we want the information has to be consistency, which means whatever information user has given, CPU should be able to see it as first as possible. That is the reason we want to disable caching. So, this bit **enables or disable** caching of the page.

7. **Modified bit** – Modified bit says whether the page has been modified or not. Modified means sometimes you might try to write something on to the page. If a page is modified, then whenever you should replace that page with some other page, then the modified information should be kept on the hard disk or it has to be written back or it has to be saved back. It is set to 1 by hardware on write-access to page which is used to avoid writing when swapped out. Sometimes this modified bit is also called as the **Dirty bit.**

Paging System Structure:

Hashed Page Tables

- Common in address spaces > 32 bits.
- The virtual page number is hashed into a page table.
- This page table contains a chain of elements hashing to the same location.
- Virtual page numbers are compared in this chain searching for a match.
- If a match is found, the corresponding physical frame is extracted.

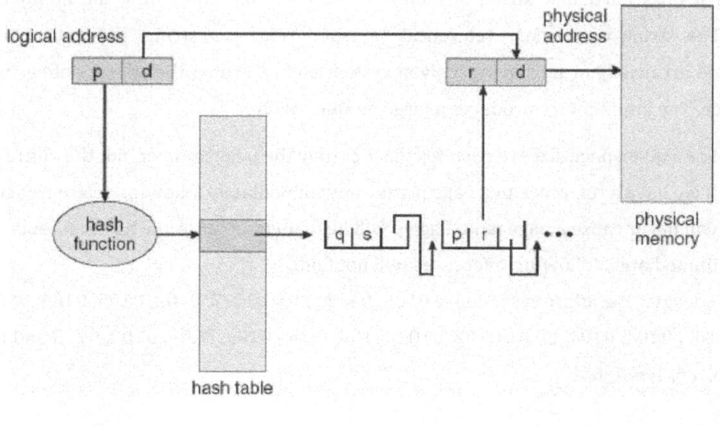

Inverted Page Table

- One entry for each real page of memory.
- Entry consists of the virtual address of the page stored in that real memory location, with information about the process that owns that page.
- Decreases memory needed to store each page table, but increases time needed to search the table when a page reference occurs.
- Use hash table to limit the search to one — or at most a few — page-table entries.

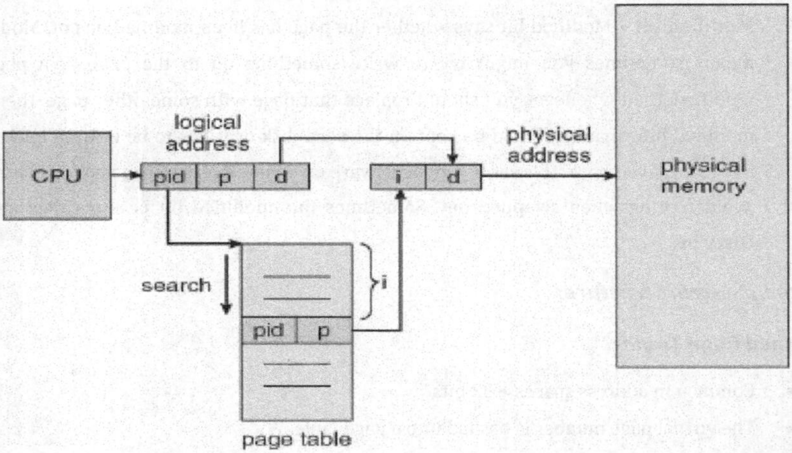

3.9. Page Replacement Algorithm

There are many different page replacement algorithms. We evaluate an algorithm by running it on a particular string of memory reference and computing the number of page faults. The string of memory references is called reference string. Reference strings are generated artificially or by tracing a given system and recording the address of each memory reference. The latter choice produces a large number of data.

1. For a given page size we need to consider only the page number, not the entire address.
2. If we have a reference to a page p, then any immediately following references to page p will never cause a page fault. Page p will be in memory after the first reference; the immediately following references will not fault.

Eg:- consider the address sequence 0100, 0432, 0101, 0612, 0102, 0103, 0104, 0101, 0611, 0102, 0103, 0104, 0101, 0610, 0102, 0103, 0104, 0104, 0101, 0609, 0102, 0105 and reduce to 1, 4, 1, 6,1, 6, 1, 6, 1, 6, 1.

To determine the number of page faults for a particular reference string and page replacement algorithm, we also need to know the number of page frames available. As the number of frames available increase, the number of page faults will decrease.

3.9.1. *FIFO Algorithm*

The simplest page-replacement algorithm is a FIFO algorithm. A FIFO replacement algorithm associates with each page the time when that page was brought into memory. When a page must be replaced, the oldest page is chosen. We can create a FIFO queue to hold all pages in memory.

The first three references (7, 0, 1) cause page faults, and are brought into these empty eg. 7, 0, 1, 2, 0, 3, 0, 4, 2, 3, 0, 3, 2, 1, 2, 0, 1 and consider 3 frames. This replacement means that the next reference to 0 will fault. Page 1 is then replaced by page 0.

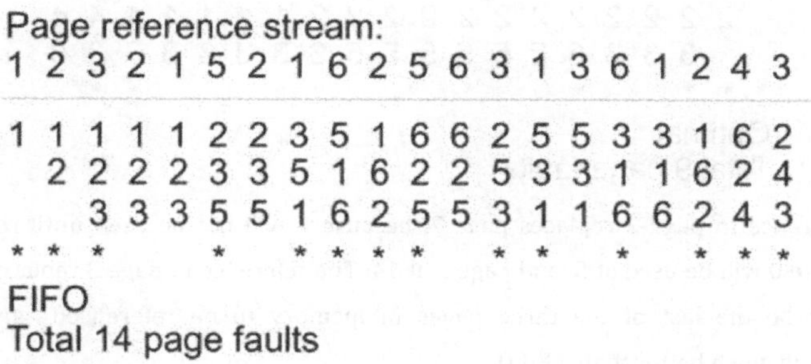

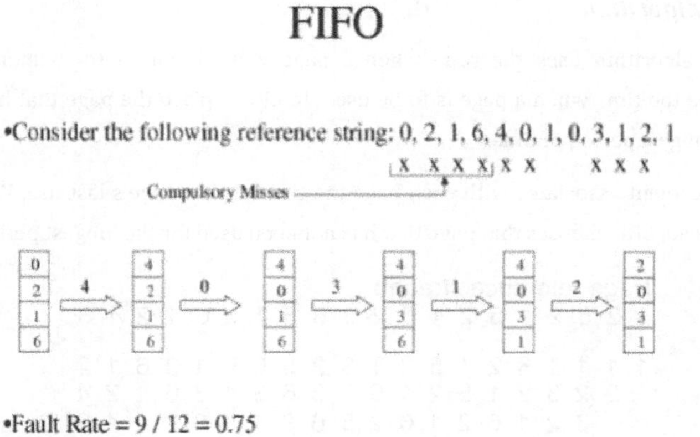

3.9.2. *Optimal Algorithm*

An optimal page-replacement algorithm has the lowest page-fault rate of all algorithms. An optimal page-replacement algorithm exists, and has been called OPT or MIN. It is simply Replace the page that will not be used for the longest period of time.

Now consider the same string with 3 empty frames.

The Belady's optimal algorithm cheats. It looks forward in time to see which frame to replace on a page fault. Thus it is not a real replacement algorithm. It gives us a frame of reference for a given static frame access sequence.

```
Page reference stream:
1 2 3 2 1 5 2 1 6 2 5 6 3 1 3 6 1 2 4 3
---------------------------------------
1 1 1 1 1 1 1 1 6 6 6 6 6 6 6 6 6 2 2 2
  2 2 2 2 2 2 2 2 2 2 2 2 1 1 1 1 1 4 4
    3 3 3 5 5 5 5 5 5 5 3 3 3 3 3 3 3 3
* * *     *     *       * *       * *
Optimal
Total 9 page faults
```

The reference to page 2 replaces page 7, because 7 will not be used until reference 18, whereas page 0 will be used at 5, and page 1 at 14. The reference to page 3 replaces page 1, as page 1 will be the last of the three pages in memory to be referenced again. Optimal replacement is much better than a FIFO.

3.9.3. *LRU Algorithm*

The FIFO algorithm uses the time when a page was brought into memory; the OPT algorithm uses the time when a page is to be used. In LRU replace the page that has not been used for the longest period of time.

LRU replacement associates with each page the time of that page's last use. When a page must be replaced, LRU chooses that page that has not been used for the longest period of time.

```
Page reference stream:
1 2 3 2 1 5 2 1 6 2 5 6 3 1 3 6 1 2 4 3
---------------------------------------
1 1 1 1 3 2 1 5 2 1 6 2 5 6 6 1 3 6 1 2
  2 2 3 2 1 5 2 1 6 2 5 6 3 1 3 6 1 2 4
    3 2 1 5 2 1 6 2 5 6 3 1 3 6 1 2 4 3
* * *     *     *   *   * *       * * *
LRU
Total 11 page faults
```

Let SR be the reverse of a reference string S, then the page-fault rate for the OPT algorithm on S is the same as the page-fault rate for the OPT algorithm on SR.

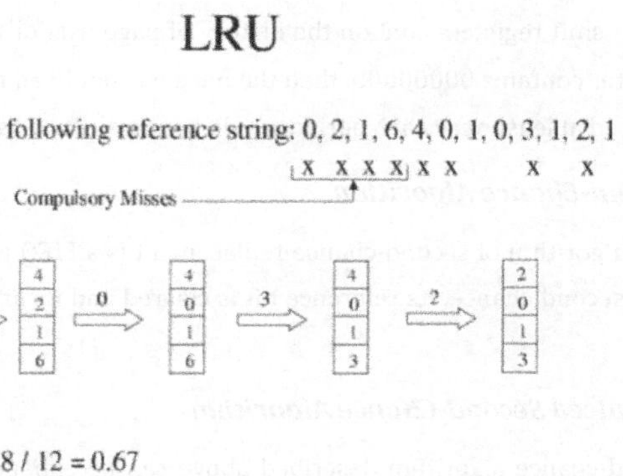

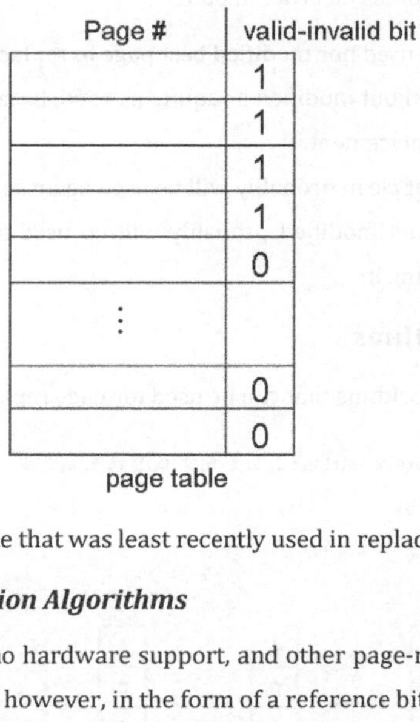

On a page fault, the frame that was least recently used in replaced.

3.9.4. LRU Approximation Algorithms

Some systems provide no hardware support, and other page-replacement algorithm. Many systems provide some help, however, in the form of a reference bit. The reference bit for a page is set, by the hardware, whenever that page is referenced. Reference bits are associated with each entry in the page table Initially, all bits are cleared (to 0) by the operating system. As a user process executes, the bit associated with each page referenced is set (to 1) by the hardware.

3.9.4.1. Additional-Reference-Bits Algorithm

The operating system shifts the reference bit for each page into the high-order or of its 8-bit byte, shifting the other bits right 1 bit, discarding the low-order bit.

These 8-bit shift registers contain the history of page use for the last eight time periods. If the shift register contains 00000000, then the page has not been used for eight time periods; a page that is used at least once each period would have a shift register value of 11111111.

3.9.4.2. Second-Chance Algorithm

The basic algorithm of second-chance replacement is a FIFO replacement algorithm. When a page gets a second chance, its reference bit is cleared and its arrival e is reset to the current time.

3.9.4.3. Enhanced Second-Chance Algorithm

The second-chance algorithm described above can be enhanced by considering troth the reference bit and the modify bit as an ordered pair.

1. (0,0) neither recently used nor modified best page to replace.
2. (0,1) not recently used but modified not quite as good, because the page will need to be written out before replacement.
3. (1,0) recently used but clean probably will be used again soon.
4. (1,1) recently used and modified probably will be used again, and write out will be needed before replacing it

3.10. Counting Algorithms

There are many other algorithms that can be used for page replacement.

Reference String : 0, 2, 1, 6, 4, 0, 1, 0, 3, 1, 2, 1

Misses :x x x x x x x x x

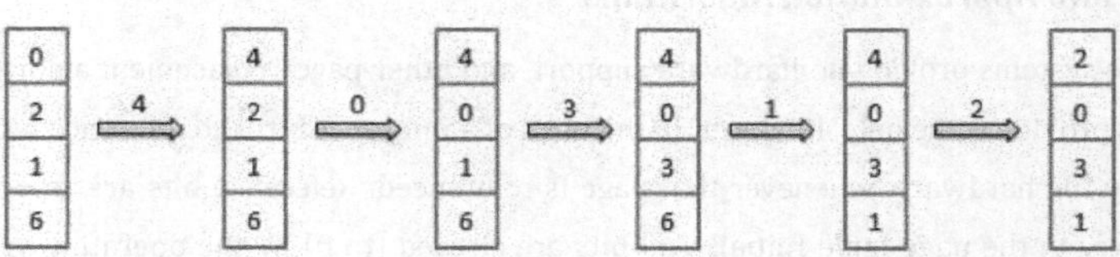

Fault Rate = 9 / 12 = 0.75

LFU Algorithm: The least frequently used (LFU) page-replacement algorithm requires that the page with the smallest count be replaced. This algorithm suffers from the situation in which a page is used heavily during the initial phase of a process, but then is never used again.

MFU Algorithm: The most frequently used (MFU) page-replacement algorithm is based on the argument that the page with the smallest count was probably just brought in and has yet to be used.

3.11. Page Buffering Algorithm

When a page fault occurs, a victim frame is chosen as before. However, the desired page is read into a free frame from the pool before the victim is written out. This procedure allows the process to restart as soon as possible, without waiting for the victim page to be written out. When the victim is later written out, its frame is added to the free-frame pool.

When the FIFO replacement algorithm mistakenly replaces a page mistakenly replaces a page that is still in active use, that page is quickly retrieved from the free-frame buffer, and no I/O is necessary. The free-frame buffer provides protection against the relatively poor, but simple, FIFO replacement algorithm.

Virtual Machines

- A virtual machine takes the layered approach to its logical conclusion. It treats hardware and the operating system kernel as though they were all hardware.
- A virtual machine provides an interface *identical* to the underlying bare hardware.
- The operating system host creates the illusion that a process has its own processor and (virtual memory).
- Each guest provided with a (virtual) copy of underlying computer.

Virtual Machines History and Benefits

- First appeared commercially in IBM mainframes in 1972.
- Fundamentally, multiple execution environments (different operating systems) can share the same hardware.
- Protect from each other.
- Some sharing of file can be permitted, controlled.
- Commutate with each other, other physical systems via networking.
- Useful for development, testing.
- Consolidation of many low-resource use systems onto fewer busier systems.

- "Open Virtual Machine Format", standard format of virtual machines, allows a VM to run within many different virtual machine (host) platforms

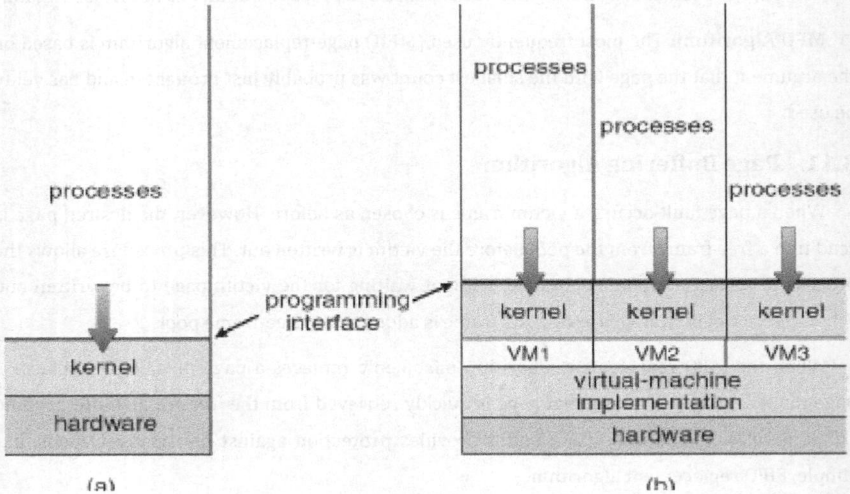

VMware Architecture

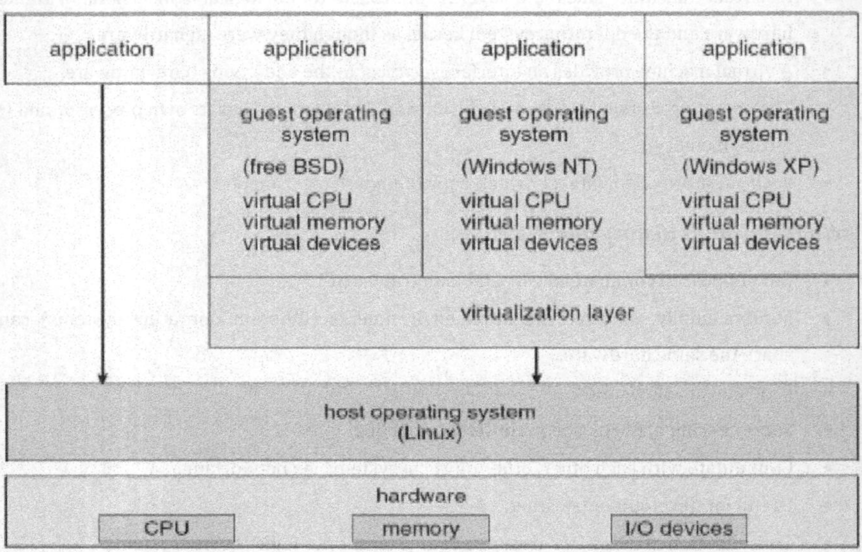

3.12. Summary

Memory management algorithms for multi programmed operating systems range from the simple single user system approach to paged segmentation. The most important determinant of the method used in a particular system is the hardware provided, every memory address generated by the CPU must be checked for legality and possibly mapped to a physical address, the checking cannot be implemented in software. Hence, we are constrained by the hardware available. The various memory management algorithms (continuous allocation, paging, segmentation, and combinations of paging and segmentation) differ in many aspects. In computing different memory management strategies, we use hardware support, performance, fragmentation, relocation, swapping, sharing and protection.

It is desirable to be able to execute a process whose logical address space larger than the available physical address space. Virtual memory is a technique that enables us to map a logical address space onto a smaller physical memory. Virtual memory allows us to run extremely large processes and to raise the degree of multiprogramming, increasing CPU utilization. Virtual memory also enables us to use an efficient type of process creation known as copy-on-write, where in parent and child processes share actual pages of memory.

Virtual memory is commonly implemented by demand paging. pure demand paging never brings in a page until that page is referenced. The first reference causes page fault to the operating system. If total memory requirements exceed the capacity of physical memory, then it may be necessary to replace pages from memory to free frames for new pages. Various page replacement algorithm are used.

In addition to a page replacement algorithm, a frame allocation policy is needed. Allocation can be fixed, suggesting local page replacement, or dynamic, suggesting global replacement.

3.13. Model Questions

- Differentiate internal and external fragmentation?
- Explain segmentation?
- What are hardware is required for paging?
- Write a note on virtual memory?
- Explain Page replacement algorithm in detail?
- Compare demand paging and segmentation?
- Explain page replacement algorithm?
- Define and explain Virtual Memory?

- Explain advantages and disadvantages Demand Paging
- Define and explain Performance of demand paging?
- Describe Page Replacement Algorithms?
- Explain various Allocation Algorithms?

3.14. Objective Questions

1. Because of virtual memory, the memory can be shared among.

   a) Processes

   b) Threads

   c) Instructions

   d) None of the mentioned

2. The pager concerns with the,

   a) Individual page of a process

   b) Entire process

   c) Entire thread

   d) First page of a process

3. When a program tries to access a page that is mapped in address space but not loaded in physical memory, then,

   a) Segmentation fault occurs

   b) Fatal error occurs

   c) Page fault occurs

   d) No error occurs

4. In FIFO page replacement algorithm, when a page must be replaced.

   a) Oldest page is chosen

   b) Newest page is chosen

   c) Random page is chosen

   d) None of the mentioned

5. A process is thrashing if,

   a) It is spending more time paging than executing

   b) It is spending less time paging than executing

   c) Page fault occurs

   d) Swapping cannot take place

6. Working set model for page replacement is based on the assumption of,

   a) Modularity

   b) Locality

   c) Globalization

   d) Random access

7. Which algorithm chooses the page that has not been used for the longest period of time whenever the page required to be replaced?

   a) First in first out algorithm

   b) Additional reference bit algorithm

   c) Least recently used algorithm

   d) Counting based page replacement algorithm

8. Effective access time is directly proportional to,

   a) Page-fault rate

   b) Hit ratio

   c) Memory access time

   d) None of the mentioned

9. Swap space exists in,

   a) Primary memory

   b) Secondary memory

   c) CPU

   d) None of the mentioned

10. ____ is the concept in which a process is copied into main memory from the secondary memory according to the requirement.

    a) Paging

    b) Demand paging

    c) Segmentation

    d) Swapping

11. CPU fetches the instruction from memory according to the value of,

    a) Program counter

    b) Status register

    c) Instruction register

    d) Program status word

12. A memory buffer used to accommodate a speed differential is called,

    a) Stack pointer

    b) Cache

    c) Accumulator

    d) Disk buffer

13. Which one of the following is the address generated by CPU?

    a) Physical address

    b) Absolute address

    c) Logical address

    d) None of the mentioned

14. Run time mapping from virtual to physical address is done by,

    a) Memory management unit

    b) CPU

    c) PCI

    d) None of the mentioned

15. Memory management technique in which system stores and retrieves data from secondary storage for use in main memory is called,

    a) Fragmentation

    b) Paging

    c) Mapping

    d) None of the mentioned

16. The address of a page table in memory is pointed by,

    a) Stack pointer

    b) Page table base register

    c) Page register

    d) Program counter

17. Program always deals with,

    a) Logical address

    b) Absolute address

    c) Physical address

    d) Relative address

18. The page table contains,

    a) Base address of each page in physical memory

    b) Page offset

    c) Page size

    d) None of the mentioned

19. What is compaction?

    a) A technique for overcoming internal fragmentation

    b) A paging technique

    c) A technique for overcoming external fragmentation

    d) A technique for overcoming fatal error

20. Operating System maintains the page table for,

    a) Each process

    b) Each thread

    c) Each instruction

    d) Each address

CHAPTER 4

STORAGE MANAGEMENT AND FILE SYSTEMS

4.1. Objective

- Describe the physical structure of secondary and tertiary storage devices and the resulting effects on the uses of the devices.
- Explain the performance characteristics of mass-storage devices.
- Discuss operating-system services provided for mass storage.
- To explain the function of file systems.
- To describe the interfaces to the file systems.
- To discuss file system design tradeoffs, including access methods, file sharing, file locking, and directory structure.
- To explore file system protection.

4.2. File Concept

- A file is a collection of similar records. The file is treated as a single entity by users and applications and may be referred by name. Files have unique file names and may be created and deleted. Restrictions on access control usually apply at the file level.
- A file is a container for a collection of information. The file manager provides a protection mechanism to allow users administrator how processes executing on behalf of different users can access the information in a file. File protection is a fundamental property of files because it allows different people to store their information on a shared computer.
- File represents programs and data. Data files may be numeric, alphabetic, binary or alpha numeric. Files may be free form, such as text files. In general, file is sequence of bits, bytes, lines or records.
- A file has a certain defined structure according to its type.
    1. Text File
    2. Source File
    3. Executable File
    4. Object File

4.3. File Structure

The terms used for files:

- Field
- Record
- Database

A field is the basic element of data. An individual field contains a single value. A record is a collection of related fields that can be treated as a unit by some application program.

A file is a collection of similar records. The file is treated as a singly entity by users and applications and may be referenced by name. Files have file names and maybe created and deleted. Access control restrictions usually apply at the file level.

A database is a collection of related data. Database is designed for use by a number of different applications. A database may contain all of the information related to an organization or project, such as a business or a scientific study. The database itself consists of one or more types of files. Usually, there is a separate database management system that is independent of the operating system.

4.4. File Attributes

File attributes vary from one operating system to another. The common attributes are,

- Name – only information kept in human-readable form.
- Identifier – unique tag (number) identifies file within file system.
- Type – needed for systems that support different types.
- Location – pointer to file location on device.
- Size – current file size.
- Protection – controls who can do reading, writing, executing.
- Time, date, and user identification – data for protection, security, and usage monitoring.
- Information about files are kept in the directory structure, which is maintained on the disk.

4.5. File Operations

Any file system provides not only a means to store data organized as files, but a collection of functions that can be performed on files. Typical operations include the following:

Create: A new file is defined and positioned within the structure of files.

Delete: A file is removed from the file structure and destroyed.

Open: An existing file is declared to be "opened" by a process, allowing the process to perform functions on the file.

Close: The file is closed with respect to a process, so that the process no longer may perform functions on the file, until the process opens the file again.

Read: A process reads all or a portion of the data in a file.

Write: A process updates a file, either by adding new data that expands the size of the file or by changing the values of existing data items in the file.

System Calls: program makes a request to the OS for a service; looks like a C function call

- see man 2 system calls.
- see man 2 open.
- **open**: system call to open a file.
- open returns a file descriptor, an integer specifiying the position of this open file in the table of open files for the current process.
- **creat**: (no 'e') system call to create a file /* no longer necessary */
- **close**: system call to close a file.
- **read**: read data from a file opened for reading.
- **write**: write data to a file opened for writing.
- **lseek**: seek to a specified position in a file (used for random access when reading or writing a file).
    - The original **seek** system call used a 16 bit address.
    - "lseek" is named because it uses a "long" integer as the address to seek to. In practice this is a 32 bit integer on most current machines.
    - The UNIX standards organizations have apparently not yet standardized a suitable seek system call for 64 bit addresses.
    - Currently (January 2005), the **llseek** system call is available on Solaris (hercules), but there is no indication that this system call is portable.
    - Versions of Linux apparently support _llseek() or llseek() for raw devices. Compilers may support lseek() as accepting a 64-bit long or add lseek64(), according to a compile-time option.

File Types – Name, Extension

A common technique for implementing file types is to include the type as part of the file name. The name is split into two parts : a name and an extension. Following table gives the file type with usual extension and function.

File Type	Usual Extension	Function
Executable	exe, com, bin	Read to run machine language program.
Object	obj, o	Compiled, machine language, not linked
Source Code	c, cc, java, pas asm, a	Source code in various language
Text	txt, doc	Textual data, documents

4.6. File Management Systems

A file management system is that set of system software that provides services to users and applications in the use of files. following objectives for a file management system:

- To meet the data management needs and requirements of the user which include storage of data and the ability to perform the aforementioned operations.
- To guarantee, to the extent possible, that the data in the file are valid.
- To optimize performance, both from the system point of view in terms of overall throughput.
- To provide I/O support for a variety of storage device types.
- To minimize or eliminate the potential for lost or destroyed data.
- To provide a standardized set of I/O interface routines to use processes.

TO provide I/O support for multiple users, in the case of multiple-user systems File System Architecture. At the lowest level, device drivers communicate directly with peripheral devices or their controllers or channels. A device driver is responsible for starting I/O operations on a device and processing the completion of an I/O request. For file operations, the typical devices controlled are disk and tape drives. Device drivers are usually considered to be part of the operating system. The I/O control, consists of device drivers and interrupt handlers to transfer information between the memory and the disk system. A device driver can be thought of as a translator.

The basic file system needs only to issue generic commands to the appropriate device driver to read and write physical blocks on the disk. The file-organization module knows about files and their logical blocks, as well as physical blocks. By knowing the type of file allocation used and the location of the file, the file-organization module can translate logical block addresses to physical block addresses for the basic file system to transfer. Each file's logical blocks are numbered from 0 (or 1) through N, whereas the physical blocks containing the data usually do not match the logical numbers, so a translation is needed to locate each block.

The file-organization module also includes the free-space manager, which tracks unallocated and provides these blocks to the file organization module when requested. The logical file system uses the directory structure to provide the file- organization module with the information the latter needs, given a symbolic file name. The logical file system is also responsible for protection and security. To create a new file, an application program calls the logical file system. The logical file system knows the format of the directory structures. To create a new file, it reads the appropriate directory into memory, updates it with the new entry, and writes it back to the disk. Once the file is found the associated information such as size, owner, access permissions and data block locations are generally copied into a table in memory, referred to as the open-file fable, consisting of information about all the currently opened files.

The first reference to a file (normally an open) causes the directory structure to be searched and the directory entry for this file to be copied into the table of opened files. The index into this table is returned to the user program, and all further references are made through the index rather than with a symbolic name. The name given to the index varies. Unix systems refer to it as a file descriptor, Windows/NT as a file handle, and other systems as a file control block. Consequently, as long as the file is not closed, all file operations are done on the open-file table. When the file is closed by all users that have opened it, the updated file information is copied back to the disk-based directory structure.

File Access Methods

The way that files are accessed and read into memory is determined by Access methods. Usually a single access method is supported by systems while there are OS's that support multiple access methods.

1. Sequential Access

- Data is accessed one record right after another is an order.
- Read command cause a pointer to be moved ahead by one.
- Write command allocate space for the record and move the pointer to the new End of File.
- Such a method is reasonable for tape.

2. Direct Access

- This method is useful for disks.
- The file is viewed as a numbered sequence of blocks or records.

- There are no restrictions on which blocks are read/written, it can be dobe in any order.
- User now says "read n" rather than "read next".
- "n" is a number relative to the beginning of file, not relative to an absolute physical disk location.

3. Indexed Sequential Access

- It is built on top of Sequential access.
- It uses an Index to control the pointer while accessing files.

4.7. File-System Mounting

- As a file must be opened before it is used, a file system must be mounted before it can be available to processes on the system. The mount procedure is straight forward. The stem is given the name of the device, and the location within the file structure at which to attach the file system (called the mount point).
- The operating system verifies that the device contains a valid file system. It does so by asking the device driver to read the device directory and verifying that the directory has the expected format. Finally, the operating system notes in its directory structure that a file system is mounted at the specified mount point. This scheme enables the operating system to traverse its directory structure, switching among file systems as appropriate.

What is a Directory?

Information about files is maintained by Directories. A directory can contain multiple files. It can even have directories inside of them. In Windows we also call these directories as folders. Following is the information maintained in a directory:

- **Name**: The name visible to user.
- **Type**: Type of the directory.
- **Location**: Device and location on the device where the file header is located.
- **Size**: Number of bytes/words/blocks in the file.
- **Position**: Current next-read/next-write pointers.
- **Protection**: Access control on read/write/execute/delete.
- **Usage**: Time of creation, access, modification etc.
- **Mounting**: When the root of one file system is "grafted" into the existing tree of another file system its called Mounting.

Allocation Methods

- The direct-access nature of disks allows us flexibility in the implementation of files. Three major methods of allocating disk space are in wide use: contiguous, linked and indexed. Each method has its advantages and disadvantages.

Contiguous Allocation

- The contiguous allocation method requires each file to occupy a set of contiguous blocks on the disk. Disk addresses define a linear ordering on the disk. Notice that with this ordering assuming that only one job is accessing the disk, accessing block b + 1 after block b normally requires no head movement. When head movement is needed, it is only one track. Thus, the number of disk seeks required for accessing contiguously allocated files is minimal.
- Contiguous allocation of a file is defined by the disk address and length (in block units) of the first block. If the file is n blocks long, and starts at location!), then it occupies blocks b, b + 1, b + 2, ..., b + n – 1. The directory entry for each file indicates the address of the starting block and the length of the area allocate for this file.
- Accessing a file that has been allocated contiguously is easy. For sequential access, the file system remembers the disk address of the last block referenced and, when necessary, reads the next block. For direct access to block i of a file that starts at block b, we can immediately access block b + i.
- The contiguous disk-space-allocation problem can be seen to be a particular application of the general dynamic storage-allocation First Fit and Best Fit are the most common strategies used to select a free hole from the set of available holes. Simulations have shown that both first-fit and best-fit are more efficient than worst-fit in terms of both time and storage utilization. Neither first-fit nor best-fit is clearly best in terms of storage utilization, but first-fit is generally faster.
- These algorithms suffer from the problem of external fragmentation. As files are allocated and deleted, the free disk space is broken into little pieces. External fragmentation exists whenever free space is broken into chunks.
- To prevent loss of significant amounts of disk space to external fragmentation, the user had to run repacking routine that copied the entire file system onto another floppy disk or onto a tape. The original floppy disk was then freed completely, creating one large contiguous free space.

- The routine then copied the files back onto the floppy disk by allocating contiguous space from this one large hole. This scheme effectively compacts all free space into one contiguous space, solving the fragmentation problem. The cost of this compaction is time. The time cost is particularly severe for large hard disks that use contiguous allocation, where compacting all the space may take hours and may be necessary on a weekly basis. During this down time, normal system operation generally cannot be permitted, so such compaction is avoided at all costs on production machines.

Contiguous Allocation of Disk Space

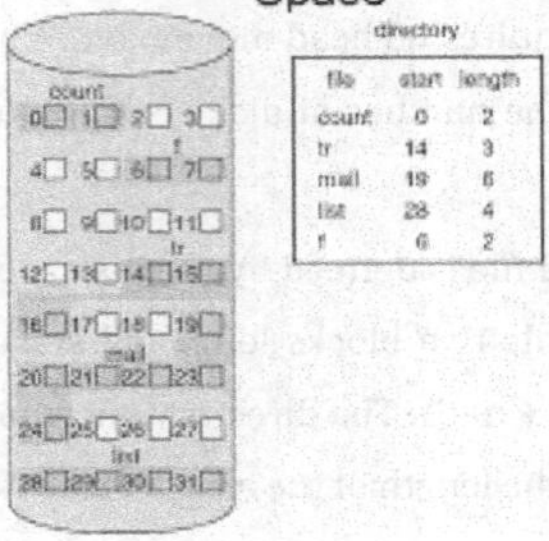

- A major problem is determining how much space is needed for a file. When the file is created, the total amount of space it will need must be found and allocated.
- The user will normally over estimate the amount of space needed, resulting in considerable wasted space.

Linked Allocations

- Linked allocation solves all problems of contiguous allocation. With link allocation, each file is a linked list disk blocks; the disk blocks may be scattered anywhere on the disk.
- This pointer is initialized to nil (the end-of-list pointer value) to signify an empty file. The size field is also set to 0. A write to the file causes a free bio to be found via the free-space management system, and this new block is the written to, and is linked to the end of the file.
- There is no external fragmentation with linked allocation, and any free! block on the free-space list can be used to satisfy a request. Notice also that there is no need to declare the size of a file when that file is created. A file can continue to grow as long as there are free blocks. Consequently, it is never necessary to compact disk space.

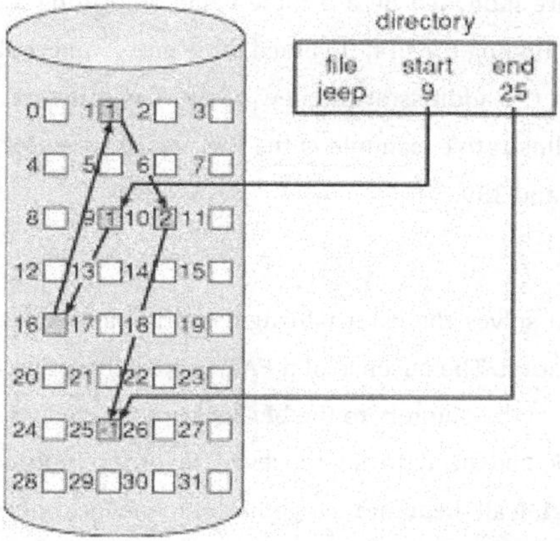

- The major problem is that it can be used effectively for only sequential access files. To find the ith block of a file we must start at the beginning of that file, and follow the pointers until we get to the ith block. Each access to a pointer requires a disk read and sometimes a disk seek. Consequently, it is inefficient to support a direct-access capability for linked allocation files. Linked allocation is the space required for the pointers If a pointer requires 4 bytes out of a 512 Byte block then 0.78 percent of the disk is being used for pointer, rather than for information.
- The usual solution to this problem is to collect blocks into multiples, called clusters, and to allocate the clusters rather than blocks. For instance, the file system define a cluster as 4 blocks and operate on the disk in only cluster units.
- Yet another problem is reliability. Since the files are linked together by pointers scattered all over the disk, consider what would happen if a pointer— were lost or damaged. Partial solutions are to use doubly linked lists or to store the file name and relative block number in each block; however, these schemes require even more overhead for each file.
- An important variation, on the linked allocation method is the use of a file allocation table (FAT). This simple but efficient method of disk-space allocation is used by the MS-DOS and OS/2 operating systems. A section of disk at the beginning of each-partition is set aside to contain the table. The table has one entry for each disk block, and is indexed by block number. The FAT is used much as is a linked list. The directory entry contains the block number of the first block of the file. The table entry indexed by that block number then contains the block number of the next block in the file. This chain continues until the last block, which has a special end-of-file value -as the table entry.

Unused blocks are indicated by a 0 table value. Allocating a new block to a file is a simple matter of finding the first 0-valued table entry, and replacing the previous end-of-file value with the address of the new block. The 0 is then replaced with the end-offile value. An illustrative example is the FAT structure of for a file consisting of disk blocks 217, 618, and 339.

Indexed Allocation

- Linked allocation solves the external-fragmentation and size-declaration problems of contiguous allocation. The absence of a FAT, linked allocation cannot support efficient direct access, since the pointers to the blocks are scattered with the blocks themselves all over the disk and need to be retrieved in order Indexed allocation solves this problem by bringing all thepointers together into one location: the index block.

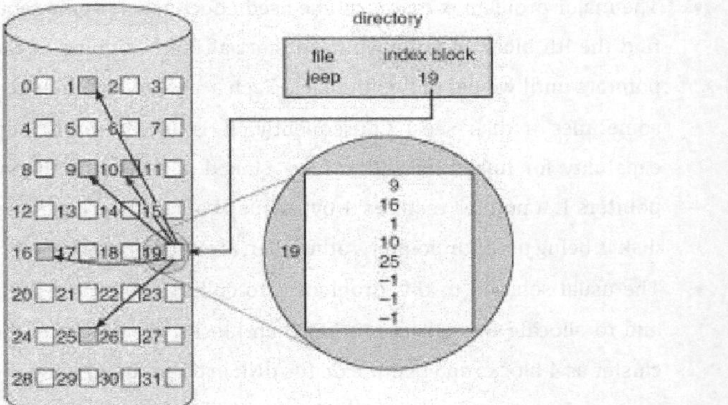

- Each file has its own index block, which is an array of disk-block addresses. The ith entry in the index block points to the ith block of the file. The directory contains the address of the index block. When the file is created, all pointers in the index block are set to nil. When the ith block is first written, a block is obtained: from the free space manager, and its address- is put in the ith index-block entry.
- Allocation supports direct access, without suffering from external fragmentation because any free block on he disk may satisfy a request for more space. Indexed allocation does suffer from wasted space. The pointer overhead of the index block is generally greater than the pointer overhead of linked allocation.

1. **Linked scheme:** An index block is normally one disk block. Thus, it can be read and written directly by itself.

2. **Multilevel index:** A variant of the linked representation is to use a first-level index block to point to a set of second-level index blocks, which in turn point to the file blocks. To access a block, the operating system uses the first-level index to find a second-level index block, and that block to find the desired data block.

Free Space Management

Since there is only a limited amount of disk space, it is necessary to reuse the space from deleted files for new files, if possible.

Bit Vector

- Free-space list is implemented as a bit map or bit vector. Each block is represented by 1 bit. If the block is free, the bit is 1; if the block is allocated, the bit is 0.
- For example consider a disk where blocks 2, 3, 4, 5, 8, 9, 10, 11, 12, 13, 17, 18, 25, 26, and 27 are free, and the rest of the blocks are allocated. The free- space bit map would be 001111001111110001100000011100000 .....

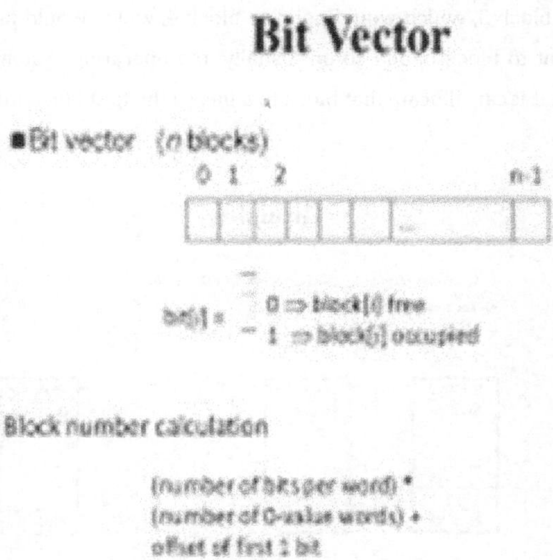

- The main advantage of this approach is that it is relatively simple and efficient to find the first free block or n consecutive free blocks on the disk.
- The calculation of the block number is (number of bits per word) x (number of 0-value words) + offset of first 1 bit.

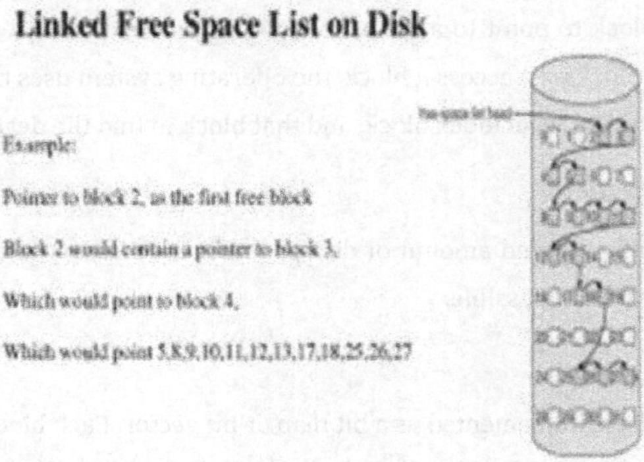

Linked List

- Another approach is to link together all the free disk blocks, keeping a pointy to the first free block in a special location on the disk and caching it in memory. This first block contains a pointer to the next free disk block, and so on. Block 2 would contain a pointer to block 3, which would point to block 4, which would point to block 5, which would point to block 8, and so on. Usually, the operating system simply needs a free block so that it can allocate that block to a file, so the first block in the free list is used.

Grouping

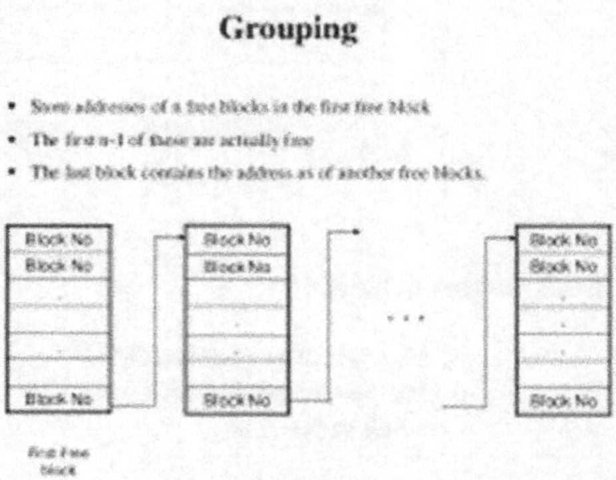

- A modification of the free-list approach is to store the addresses of n free blocks in the first free block. The first n-1 of these blocks are actually free. The importance of this implementation is that the addresses of a large number of free blocks can be found quickly, unlike in the standard linked-list approach.

Counting

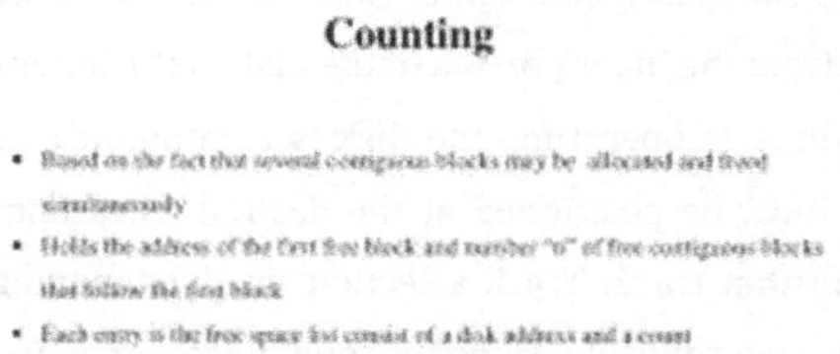

- Several contiguous blocks may be allocated or freed simultaneously, particularly when space is allocated with the contiguous allocation algorithm or through clustering. A list of n free disk addresses, we can keep the address of the first free block and the number n of free contiguous blocks that follow the first block.
- Each entry in the free-space list then consists of a disk address and a count. Although each entry requires more space than would a simple disk address, the overall list will be shorter, as long as count is generally greater than 1.

4.8. Disk Structure

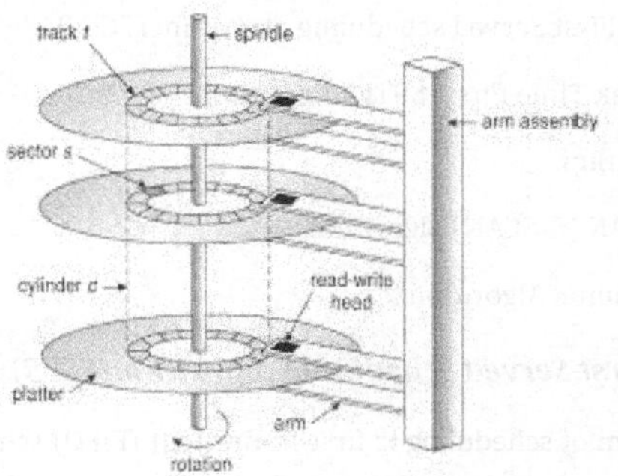

- Disk provide bulk of secondary storage of computer system. The disk can be considered the one I/O device that is common to each and every computer. Disks come in many size and speeds, and information may be stored optically or magnetically. Magnetic tape was used as an early secondary storage medium, but the access time is much slower than for disks. For backup, tapes are currently used.
- Modern disk drives are addressed as large one dimensional arrays of logical blocks, where the logical block is the smallest unit of transfer. The actual details of disk I/O operation depends on the computer system, the operating system and the nature of the I/O channel and disk controller hardware.

- The basic unit of information storage is a sector. The sectors are stored on a flat, circular, media disk. This media spins close to one or more read/write heads. The heads can move from the inner portion of the disk to the outer portion.
- When the disk drive is operating, the disk is rotating at constant speed. To read or write, the head must be positioned at the desired track and at the beginning of the desired sector on that track. Track selection involves moving the head in a movable head system or electronically selecting one head on a fixed head system. These characteristics are common to floppy disks, hard disks, CD-ROM and DVD.

4.9. Disk Scheduling

- The amount of head needed to satisfy a series of I/O request can affect the performance. If desired disk drive and controller are available, the request can be serviced immediately. If a device or controller is busy, any new requests for service will be placed on the queue of pending requests for that drive. When one request is completed, the operating system chooses which pending request to service next.
- Different types of scheduling algorithms are as follows.
    1. First Come, First Served scheduling algorithm (FCFS).
    2. Shortest Seek Time First (SSTF) algorithm.
    3. SCAN algorithm.
    4. Circular SCAN (C-SCAN) algorithm.
    5. Look Scheduling Algorithm.

4.9.1. First Come, First Served Scheduling Algorithm(FCFS)

- The simplest form of scheduling is first-in-first-out (FIFO) scheduling, which processes items from the queue in sequential order. This strategy has the advantage of being fair, because every request is honoured and the requests are honoured in the order received. With FIFO, if there are only a few processes that require access and if many of the requests are to clustered file sectors, then we can hope for good performance.
- **Priority** With a system based on priority (PRI), the control of the scheduling is outside the control of disk management software.
- **Last In First Out** In transaction processing systems, giving the device to the most recent user should result. In little or no arm movement for moving through a sequential file. Taking advantage of this locality improves throughput and reduces queue length.

4.9.2. Shortest Seek Time First (SSTF) Algorithm

- The SSTF policy is to select the disk I/O request the requires the least movement of the disk arm from its current position. Scan With the exception of FIFO, all of the policies described so far can leave some request unfulfilled until the entire queue is emptied. That is, there may always be new requests arriving that will be chosen before an existing request.
- The choice should provide better performance than FCFS algorithm.
- Under heavy load, SSTF can prevent distant request from ever being serviced. This phenomenon is known as starvation. SSTF scheduling is essentially a from of shortest job first scheduling. SSTF scheduling algorithm are not very popular because of two reasons.
    1. Starvation possibly exists.
    2. It increases higher overheads.

4.9.3. SCAN Scheduling Algorithm

- The scan algorithm has the head start at track 0 and move towards the highest numbered track, servicing all requests for a track as it passes the track. The service direction is then reserved and the scan proceeds in the opposite direction, again picking up all requests in order.
- SCAN algorithm is guaranteed to service every request in one complete pass through the disk. SCAN algorithm behaves almost identically with the SSTF algorithm. The SCAN algorithm is sometimes called elevator algorithm.

4.9.4. C SCAN Scheduling Algorithm

- The C-SCAN policy restricts scanning to one direction only. Thus, when the last track has been visited in one direction, the arm is returned to the opposite end of the disk and the scan begins again.
- This reduces the maximum delay experienced by new requests.

4.9.5. Look Scheduling Algorithm

- Start the head moving in one direction. Satisfy the request for the closest track in that direction when there is no more request in the direction, the head is traveling, reverse direction and repeat. This algorithm is similar to innermost and outermost track on each circuit.

Examples of Disk Scheduling Algorithms

These algorithms are not hard to understand, but they can confuse someone because they are so similar. What we are striving for by using these algorithms is keeping Head Movements (# tracks) to the least amount as possible. The less the head has to move the faster the seek time will be. I will show you and explain to you why C-LOOK is the best algorithm to use in trying to establish less seek time.

Given the following queue -- 95, 180, 34, 119, 11, 123, 62, 64 with the Read-write head initially at the track 50 and the tail track being at 199 let us now discuss the different algorithms.

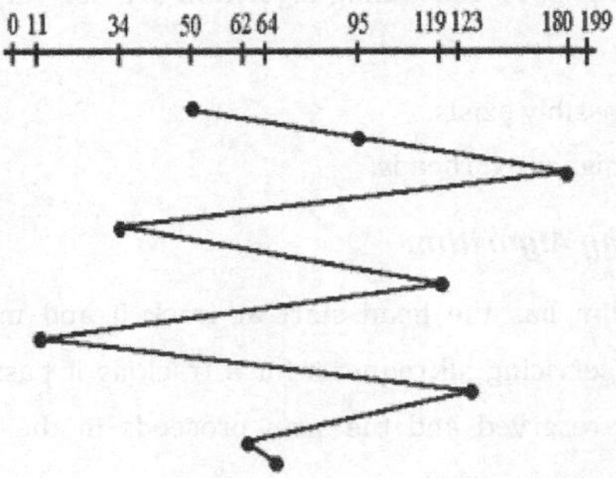

1. First Come -First Serve (FCFS): All incoming requests are placed at the end of the queue. Whatever number that is next in the queue will be the next number served. Using this algorithm doesn't provide the best results. To determine the number of head movements you would simply find the number of tracks it took to move from one request to the next. For this case it went from 50 to 95 to 180 and so on. From 50 to 95 it moved 45 tracks. If you tally up the total number of tracks you will find how many tracks it had to go through before finishing the entire request. In this example, it had a total head movement of 640 tracks. The disadvantage of this algorithm is noted by the oscillation from track 50 to track 180 and then back to track 11 to 123 then to 64. As you will soon see, this is the worse algorithm that one can use.

Consider the following disk request sequence for a disk with 100 tracks 45, 21, 67, 90, 4, 50, 89, 52, 61, 87, 25

Head pointer starting at 50 and moving in left direction. Find the number of head movements in cylinders using FCFS scheduling.

Solution

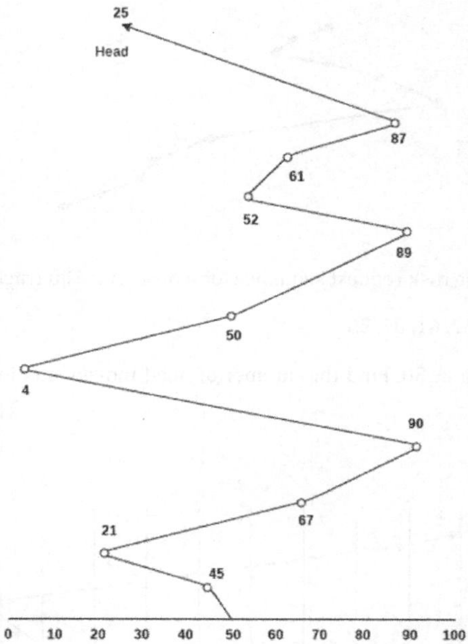

Number of cylinders moved by the head

= (50-45)+(45-21)+(67-21)+(90-67)+(90-4)+(50-4)+(89-50)+(61-52)+(87-61)+(87-25)

= 5 + 24 + 46 + 23 + 86 + 46 + 49 + 9 + 26 + 62

= 376

2. Shortest Seek Time First (SSTF): In this case request is serviced according to next shortest distance. Starting at 50, the next shortest distance would be 62 instead of 34 since it is only 12 tracks away from 62 and 16 tracks away from 34. The process would continue until all the process are taken care of.

For example the next case would be to move from 62 to 64 instead of 34 since there are only 2 tracks between them and not 18 if it were to go the other way. Although this seems to be a better service being that it moved a total of 236 tracks, this is not an optimal one. There is a great chance that starvation would take place. The reason for this is if there were a lot of requests close to each other the other requests will never be handled since the distance will always be greater.

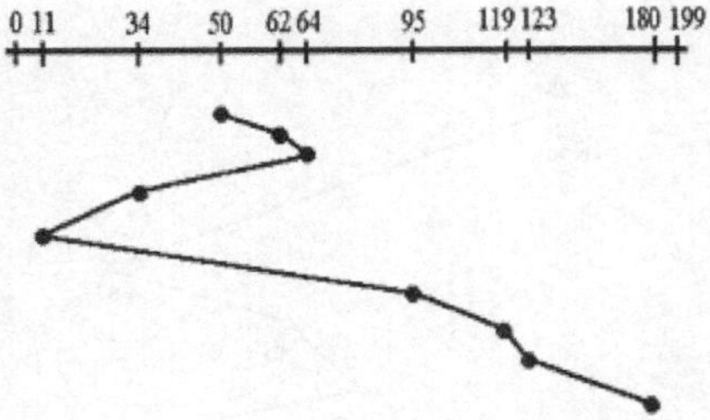

Consider the following disk request sequence for a disk with 100 tracks,

45, 21, 67, 90, 4, 89, 52, 61, 87, 25

Head pointer starting at 50. Find the number of head movements in cylinders using SSTF scheduling.

Solution

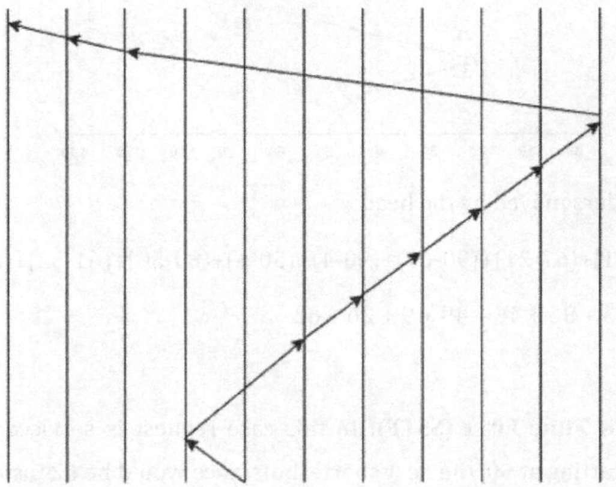

Number of cylinders = 5 + 7 + 9 + 6 + 20 + 2 + 1 + 65 + 4 + 17 = 136

3. Elevator (SCAN): This approach works like an elevator does. It scans down towards the nearest end and then when it hits the bottom it scans up servicing the requests that it didn't get going down. If a request comes in after it has been scanned it will not be serviced until the process comes back down or moves back up. This process moved a total of 230 tracks. Once again this is more optimal than the previous algorithm, but it is not the bestConsider the following disk request sequence for a disk with 100 tracks,

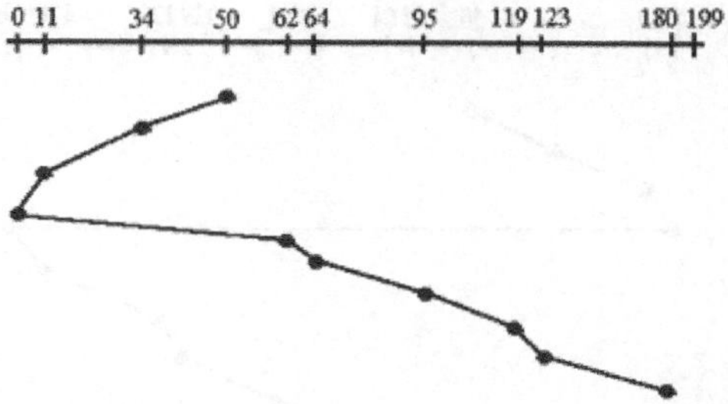

98, 137, 122, 183, 14, 133, 65, 78

Head pointer starting at 54 and moving in left direction. Find the number of head movements in cylinders using SCAN scheduling.

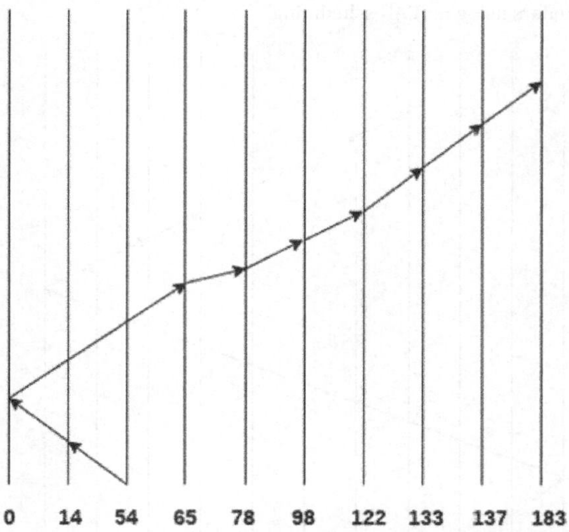

Number of Cylinders = 40 + 14 + 65 + 13 + 20 + 24 + 11 + 4 + 46 = 237

4. Circular Scan (C-SCAN): Circular scanning works just like the elevator to some extent. It begins its scan toward the nearest end and works it way all the way to the end of the system. Once it hits the bottom or top it jumps to the other end and moves in the same direction. Keep in mind that the huge jump doesn't count as a head movement. The total head movement for this algorithm is only 187 track, but still this isn't the mose sufficient. Consider the following disk request sequence for a disk with 100 tracks,

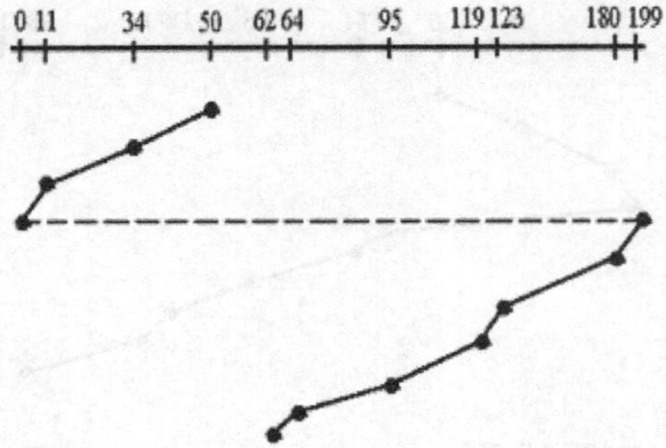

98, 137, 122, 183, 14, 133, 65, 78

Head pointer starting at 54 and moving in left direction. Find the number of head movements in cylinders using C-SCAN scheduling.

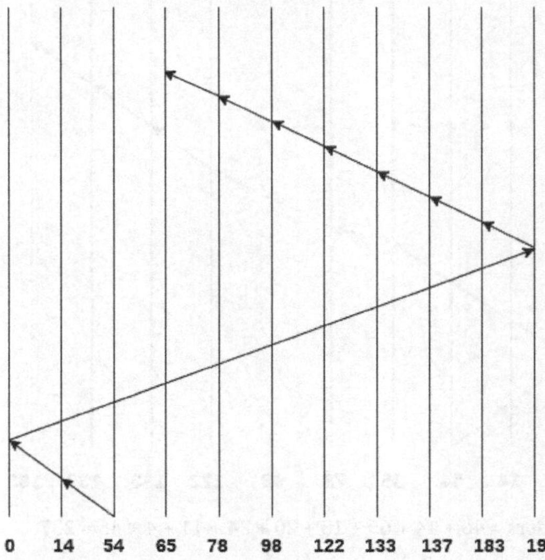

No. of cylinders crossed = 40 + 14 + 199 + 16 + 46 + 4 + 11 + 24 + 20 + 13 = 387

5. C-LOOK: This is just an enhanced version of C-SCAN. In this the scanning doesn't go past the last request in the direction that it is moving. It too jumps to the other end but not all the way to the end. Just to the furthest request. C-SCAN had a total movement of 187 but this scan (C-LOOK) reduced it down to 157 tracks.

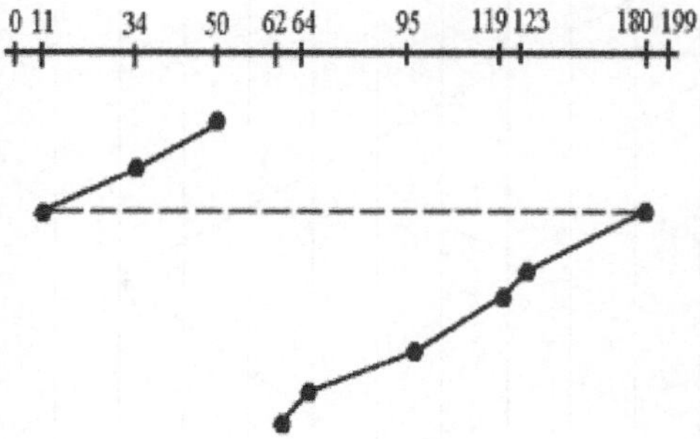

From this you were able to see a scan change from 644 total head movements to just 157. You should now have an understanding as to why your operating system truly relies on the type of algorithm it needs when it is dealing with multiple processes. Consider the following disk request sequence for a disk with 100 tracks,

98, 137, 122, 183, 14, 133, 65, 78

Head pointer starting at 54 and moving in left direction. Find the number of head movements in cylinders using LOOK scheduling.

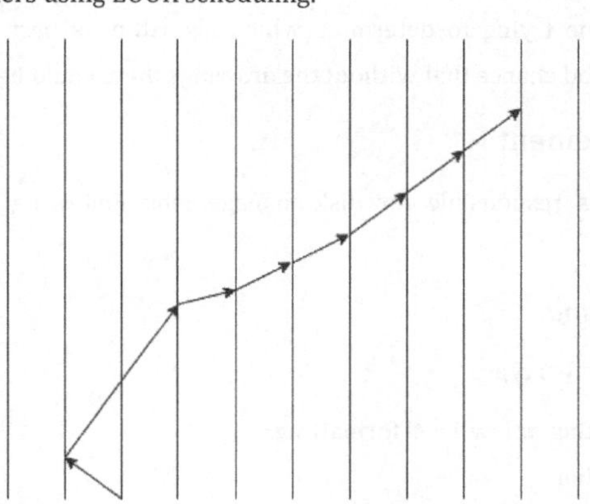

Number of cylinders crossed = 40 + 51 + 13 + +20 + 24 + 11 + 4 + 46 = 209

Consider the following disk request sequence for a disk with 100 tracks

98, 137, 122, 183, 14, 133, 65, 78

Head pointer starting at 54 and moving in left direction. Find the number of head movements in cylinders using CLOOK scheduling.

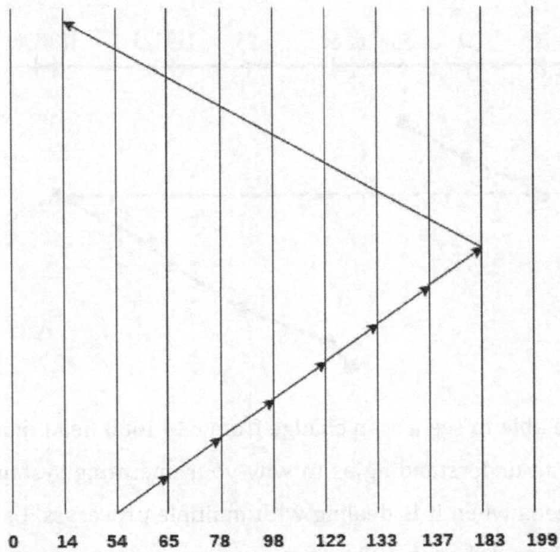

Number of cylinders crossed = 11 + 13 + 20 + 24 + 11 + 4 + 46 + 169 = 298

Note

It is important that you draw out the sequence when handling algorithms like this one. One would have a hard time trying to determine which algorithm is best by just reading the definition. There is a good chance that without the drawings there could be miscalculations.

4.10. Disk Management

Operating system is responsible for disk management. Following are some activities discussed.

4.10.1. Disk Formatting

Disk formatting is of two types.

a) Physical formatting or low-level formatting.

b) Logical Formatting.

Physical Formatting

- Disk must be formatted before storing data.
- Disk must be divided into sectors that the disk controllers can read/write.
- Low level formatting files the disk with a special data structure for each sector.
- Data structure consists of three fields: header, data area and trailer.
- Header and trailer contain information used by the disk controller.

- Sector number and Error Correcting Codes (ECC) contained in the header and trailer.
- For writing data to the sector – ECC is updated.
- For reading data from the sector – ECC is recalculated.
- Low level formatting is done at factory.

Logical Formatting

- After disk is partitioned, logical formatting used.
- Operating system stores the initial file system data structures onto the disk.

4.10.2. Boot Block

- When a computer system is powered up or rebooted, a program in read only memory executes.
- Diagnostic check is done first.
- Stage 0 boot program is executed.
- Boot program reads the first sector from the boot device and contains a stage-1 boot program.
- May be boot sector will not contain a boot program.
- PC booting from hard disk, the boot sector also contains a partition table.
- The code in the boot ROM instructs the disk controller to read the boot blocks into memory and then starts executing that code.
- Full boot strap program is more sophisticated than the bootstrap loader in the boot ROM.

4.11. Swap Space Management

Swap space management is low level task of the operating system. The main goal for the design and implementation of swap space is to provide the best throughput for the virtual memory system.

4.11.1. Swap-Space Use

The operating system needs to release sufficient main memory to bring in a process that is ready to execute.

Operating system uses this swap space in various way. Paging systems may simply store pages that have been pushed out of main memory. Unix operating system allows the use of multiple swap space are usually put on separate disks, so the load placed on the I/O system by paging and swapping can be spread over the systems I/O devices.

4.11.2. Swap Space Location

- Swap space can reside in two places:
  1. Separate disk partition
  2. Normal file System
- If the swap space is simply a large file within the file system, normal file system routines can be used to create it, name it and allocate its space. This is easy to implement but also inefficient. External fragmentation can greatly increase swapping times. Catching is used to improve the system performance. Block of information is cached in the physical memory, and by using special tools to allocate physically continuous blocks for the swap file.
- Swap space can be created in a separate disk partition. No file system or directory structure is placed on this space. A separate swap space storage manager is used to allocate and deallocate the blocks. This manager uses algorithms optimized for speed. Internal fragmentation may increase. Some operating systems are flexible and can swap both in raw partitions and in file system space.

4.12. Stable Storage Implementation

- The write ahead log, which required the availability of stable storage.
- By definition, information residing in stable storage is never lost.
- To implement such storage, we need to replicate the required information on multiple storage devices (usually disks) with independent failure modes.
- We also need to coordinate the writing of updates in a way that guarantees that a failure during an update will not leave all the copies in a damaged state and that, when we are recovering from failure, we can force all copies to a consistent and correct value, even if another failure occurs during the recovery.

4.13. Disk Reliability

- Good performance means high speed, another important aspect of performance is reliability.
- A fixed disk drive is likely to be more reliable than a removable disk or tape drive.
- An optical cartridge is likely to be more reliable than a magnetic disk or tape.
- A head crash in a fixed hard disk generally destroys the data, whereas the failure of a tape drive or optical disk drive often leaves the data cartridge unharmed.

4.14. Raid Levels

RAID stands for redundant array of independent disks. The name indicates that the disk drives are independent, and are multiple in number. How the data is distributed between these drives depends on the RAID level used.

The main advantage of RAID, is the fact that, to the operating system the array of disks can be presented as a single disk.

RAID is fault tolerant because in most of the RAID level's data is redundant in multiple disks, so even if one disk fails, or even two sometimes, the data will be safe and the operating system will not be even aware of the failure. DATA loss is prevented due to the fact that data can be recovered from the disk that are not failed.

Let's understand different terminologies that are used in RAID before getting inside different levels of RAID.

What is Stripping in RAID

Writing data on a single disk is slower, but writing data by spreading it on multiple disks is faster(because data is written in small chunks to different disks, and also fetched in small chunks by different disks)

When data is fetched from different disks, the CPU does not have to wait, because the throughput will be a combined one of all the disks.

Each and every disk drives are partitioned in small chunks (ranges from 4kb to 512kb sometimes).

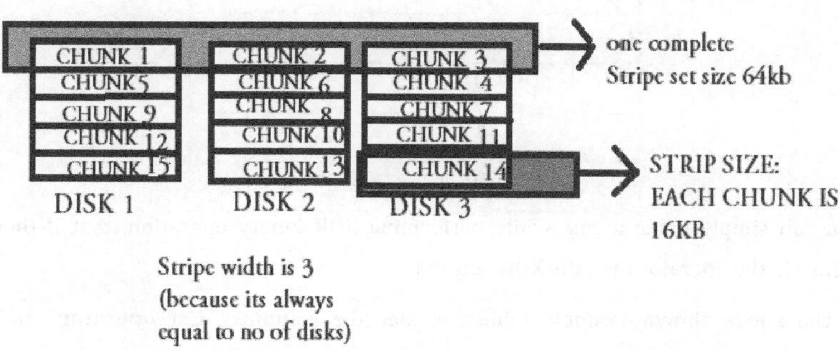

In the above shown example diagram you can see that all three disks contains different data (data that needs to be stored, will be striped in chunks and will be spreaded across different disks). There is no redundancy in this method, but is better known for high performance.

What is Mirroring in Raid?

Mirroring is a mechanism in which the same data is written to another disk drive. The main advantage of mirroring (multiple sets of same data on two disks), is that it provides 100 percent redundancy.

Suppose there are two drives in mirroring mode, then both of them will contain an exact same copy of data. So even if one disk fails, the data is safe on the other.

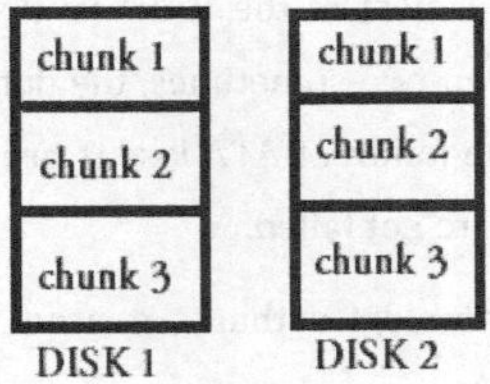

What is Parity in Raid?

Parity is an interesting method used to rebuild data in case of failure of one of the disks. Although its interesting to understand, how parity works, you will find less documentation about it on the internet.

Parity makes use of a very famous mathematical binary operation called as "XOR".

XOR is a mathematical operation that's done to produce one output from two input. Some examples of XOR operations are as below.

1'st operator	2'nd operator	XOR OUPUT
1	1	0
1	0	1
0	1	1
0	0	0

You can simply make a rule while performing XOR binary operation, that if there is a difference in the operator then the XOR output is 1.

In the above shown example table consider the columns **"1'st operator"** and **"2nd operator"** as hard disks in a RAID array, and the third column **"XOR OUPUT"** as a parity disk.

And now if one of the disk fails, you can easily construct the data on the failed disk with the help of the parity disk and the other disk which is not failed.

Parity in raid can be of two types.

1. Dedicated Parity(XOR of data bits on a dedicated parity disk)
2. Distributed Parity(XOR of data bits distributed across all data disks)

RAID 5 does a distributed parity so it can survive one disk failure.

RAID 5 does a double distributed parity so it can service two disk failures.

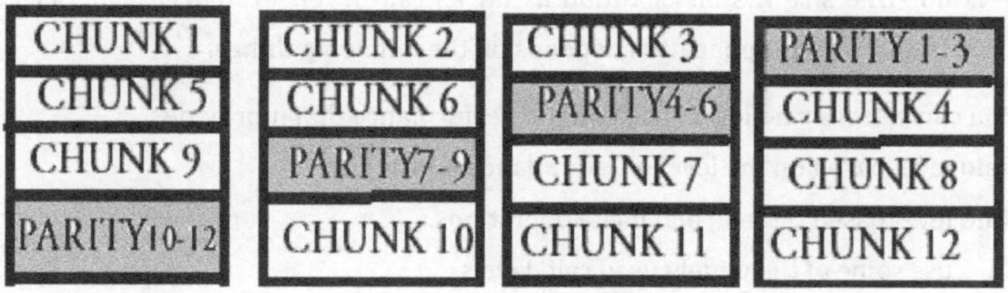

If you notice the above picture that depicts distributed parity, if suppose one disk is failed, you can build the data in it with the parity data of other disk.

Which means one stripe on one of the disk, while storing data will be used for parity of the data in other disks.

So if a disk fails, data can be reconstructed from other disk parity, and parity blocks can also be reconstructed from other disk's data.

What are Hot Spares in Raid?

Hot Spare is an extra drive added to the disk array, to increase the fault tolerance. If you have a hot spare in your Raid disk array, the Raid controller will automatically start rebuilding data on to that hot spare drive, if one of the disk from the array fails.

Which means the hot spare will automatically take the role of the failed drive once data rebuilding is complete.

You can later on replace your failed drive.

RAID management software's will provide you with a mechanism to specify the hot spare drive for your array.

What is Hot Swap in Raid?

Hot swapping is a term used to describe the ability to replace a failed disk drive without rebooting the machine.

Or in other words, hot swapping enabled you to replace a component without interrupting the normal operation of a server machine.

Different Levels of Raid

RAID (redundant array of independent disks), can be classified to different levels based on its operation and level of redundancy provided.

There is no "One size fits all" solution as far as raid levels are concerned. Selecting the suitable raid level for your application depends on the following things.

- You can select a raid level based on the performance that it provides.
- Raid level based on the level of redundancy it provides.
- Raid level based on read and write operations.

Let's discuss some of the widely used raid levels.

RAID 0 or No RAID

If your main priority is performance, then raid 0 fits right.

An important fact that should be kept in mind is that, RAID 0 does not provide any kind of redundancy. Which means even if one drive fails, your data is at risk.

It is simply striping done on your disk array. Data is broken into smaller chunks and are spread across the number of disks you have.

It has no mirroring, no parity(which means no redundancy !)

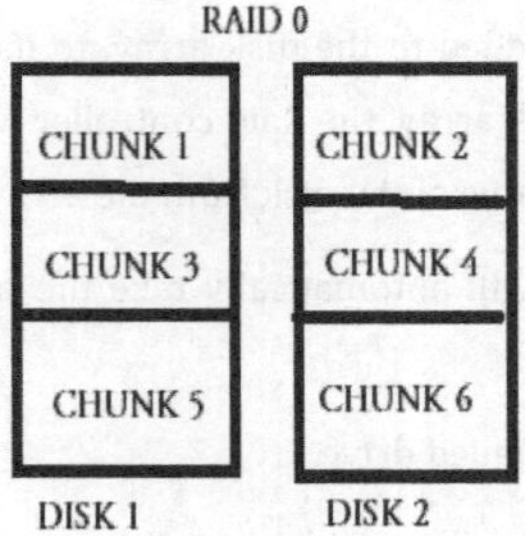

In fact raid level 0 is not RAID, because raid was primarily build for redundancy, and raid 0 does not provide any kind of redundancy, although it provides high performance.

Raid level 1(RAID 1)

RAID 1 implements heavy use of mirroring. All data in the drive is duplicated to another drive. It can be used in a situation where fault tolerance is of primary importance.

Maximum number of drives in RAID 1 can be 32, from a starting number of 2(even number of disks are required.)

Striping and parity are not used in RAID 1

You can refer the diagram shown in mirroring of raid section in this article, for RAID 1.

Raid Level 5(RAID 5)

RAID level 5 uses striping, so data is spread across number of disks used in the array, and also provides redundancy with the help of parity.

RAID 5 is a best cost effective solution for both performance and redundancy. Striped method of storing data always improves performance, and parity used in this level of raid is distributed parity.

Minimum number of disks required for raid 5 is 3, and maximum can go upto 32(depending on the RAID controller used.)

One important fact to note is that, reading rate in raid 5 is much better than writing. This is because reading can be done, by a combined rate of all disks used.

As a reference you can have a look at the distributed parity diagram shown in the **Parity in Raid section** of this article.

Raid Level 6 (RAID 6)

Raid level 6 is very much similar to raid level 5, but it has got one more added advantage.

The added advantage is that it can sustain 2 drive failures instead of 1. This is achieved again with the help of parity. In raid level 6, double distributed parity is used to achieve this level of redundancy.

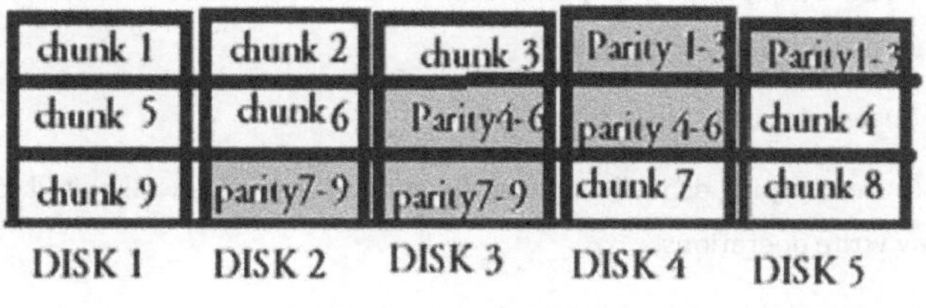

You can cleary see in the above diagram, each and every stripe set contains two parity on multiple disks. So even even if two disks gets failed at one time, data can still be recreated.

Performance of raid 6 is very much similar to performance of raid 5, its much well suited for reads that writes.

Raid 10 (Combination of Raid 0 and Raid 1)

Raid 10 is a good solution that will give you both the performance advantage of raid 0 and also the redundancy of raid 1 mirroring.

Raid 10 was made by a combination of raid 0 and raid 1. And hence you get qualities of both the raid levels.

Lets understand how data is stored in raid 10 array.

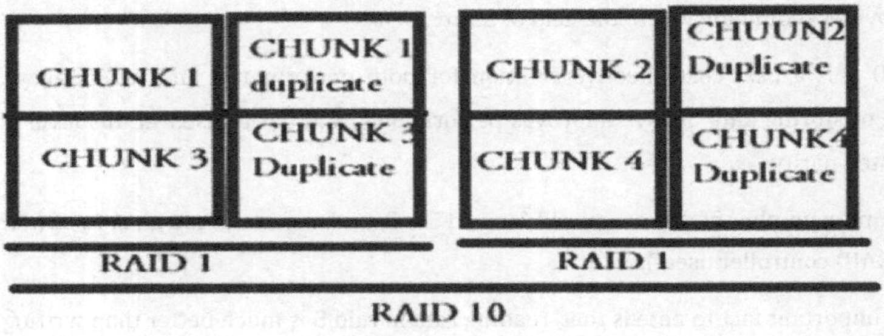

If you see the above diagram data is redundant with a duplicate set in raid 1, and also is stripped across multiple raid 1 groups to achieve performance.

This is best suitable for heavy IO usage & also provides 100 percent redundancy. Minimum number of drives required is 4. It is quite expensive, as you can clearly see that you are dedicating one disk per raid 1 array for redundancy.

But is an excellent choice for both performance and redundancy.

Summary of Different RAID Levels

- RAID 0 uses striping for high performance. Raid 0 cannot be considered as RAID as it does not provide fault tolerance.
- RAID 1 uses mirroring for redundancy.
- RAID 5 uses striping as well as parity for redundancy. It is well suited for heavy read and low write operations.
- RAID 6 uses striping and double parity for redundancy.
- RAID 10 is a combination of raid 1 and raid 0. It also provides heavy redundancy because of mirroring, and also provides performance as the data is striped across multiple raid 1 groups.

4.15. Summary

Disk drives are the major secondary storage I/O devices on most computers. Most secondary devices are either magnetic disks or magnetic tapes. Modern disk drives are structured as large one dimensional arrays of logical disk blocks. Disk scheduling algorithms can improve the effective bandwidth, the average response time, and the variance response time. Algorithms such as SSTF, SCAN, C-SCAN. LOOK, and CLOOK are designed to make such improvements through strategies for disk queue ordering.

Performance can be harmed by external fragmentation. The operating system manages block. First, a disk must be low level formatted to create the sectors on the raw hardware, new disks usually come preformatted. Then, disk is partitioned, file systems are created, and boot blocks are allocated to store the system bootstrap program. Finally when a block is corrupted, the system must have a way to lock out that block or to replace it logically with a space.

Because of efficient swap space is a key to good performance, systems usually bypass the file system and use raw disk access for paging I/O. Some systems dedicate a raw disk partition to swap space, and others use a file within the file system instead.

A file is an abstract data type defined and implemented by the operating system. It is a sequence of logical records. A logical record may be a byte, a line, or a more complex data item. The operating system may specifically support various record types or may leave that support to the application program. The major task for the operating system is to map the logical file concept onto physical storage devices such as magnetic tape or disk. All the file information kept in the directory structure. File system is implemented on the disk and memory.

Disk address define a linear addressing on the disk. Continuous allocation algorithm suffers from the external fragmentation. Free space management techniques are bit vector, linked list. Grouping, counting. Since file are the main information storage mechanism in most computer systems, file protection is needed. Access to files can be controlled separately for each type of access – read, write, execute, append, delete, list directory, and so on. File protection can be provided by access lists, passwords, or other techniques.

4.16. Model Questions

1. Explain disk structure?
2. Explain following scheduling algorithms:
3. First Come, First Served scheduling algorithm (FCFS).
4. Shortest Seek Time First (SSTF) algorithm

5. SCAN algorithm
6. Circular SCAN (C-SCAN) algorithm
7. Look Scheduling Algorithm
8. Explain swap space management?
9. Explain Disk management and types?
10. Describe disk reliability?
11. Explain the file concept?
12. List the different types of files?
13. Describe the different types of access methods?
14. What are the advantages and disadvantages of continuous, linked and indexed allocation methods?
15. Explain the file system structure?
16. What are different types of partitions and mounting?

4.17. Objective Questions

1. Which one of the following is not a secondary storage?

   a) Magnetic disks

   b) Magnetic tapes

   c) RAM

   d) None of the mentioned

2. The time for the disk arm to move the heads to the cylinder containing the desired sector is called.

   a) Disk time

   b) Seek time

   c) Arm time

   d) Sector time

3. Which private network uses storage protocol rather than networking protocol?

   a) Storage area network

   b) Local area network

   c) Wide area network

   d) None of the mentioned

4. Which algorithm of disk scheduling selects the request with the least seek time from the current head positions?

   a) SSTF scheduling

   b) FCFS scheduling

   c) SCAN scheduling

   d) LOOK scheduling

5. A swap space can reside in,

   a) Separate disk partition

   b) RAM

   c) Cache

   d) None of the mentioned

6. Operating system is responsible for,

   a) Disk initialization

   b) Booting from disk

   c) Bad-block recovery

   d) All of the mentioned

7. When we write something on the disk, which one of the following can not happen?

   a) Successful completion

   b) Partial failure

   c) Total failure

   d) None of the mentioned

8. RAID level 1 refers to,

   a) Disk arrays with striping

   b) Disk mirroring

   c) Both disk arrays with striping and disk mirroring

   d) None of the mentioned

9. The replacement of a bad block generally is not totally automatic because

   a) Data in bad block can't be replaced.

   b) Data in bad block is usually lost

   c) Bad block does not contain any data

   d) None of the mentioned

10. During recovery from a failure.

    a) Each pair of physical blocks is examined

    b) Specified pair of physical blocks is examined

    c) First pair of physical blocks is examined

    d) None of the mentioned

11. MFD stands for?

    a) Main File Directory

    b) Memory File Directory

    c) Master File Directory

    d) Master Format Directory

12. The users are allowed to read information in directories.

    a) True

    b) False

13. __________ is created when a user opens an account in the computer system.

    a) RFD

    b) Subdirectory

    c) MFD

    d) SFD

14. Two or three characters appended to relative filename separated by a period.

    a) Status

    b) Identifier

    c) Extension

    d) Descriptor

15. Files that maintain the hierarchical structure of the file system.

    a) Descriptors

    b) Directories

    c) Modifiers

    d) Relative files

16. Files in which users store information?

    a) Info files

    b) Ordinary files

    c) Special files

    d) Complex files

17. The files that appear as entries in the directories.

    a) Ordinary files

    b) Special files

    c) Duplicate files

    d) Sub directories

18. Number of regions of the disk in a UNIX files management system.

    a) 1

    b) 2

    c) 3

    d) 4

19. Several instructions execution simultaneously in _______

    a) Processing

    b) Parallel processing

    c) Serial processing

    d) Multitasking.

CHAPTER 5

DEADLOCK &SECURITY IN OS

5.1. Objectives

- To develop a description of deadlocks, which prevent sets of concurrent processes from completing their tasks.
- To present number of different methods for preventing or avoiding deadlocks in a computer system.
- To discuss security threats and attacks.
- To explain the fundamentals of encryption, authentication, and hashing.
- To examine the uses of cryptography in computing.
- To describe the various countermeasures to security attacks.

5.2. Introduction

In a multiprogramming environment, several processes may compete for a finite number of resources. A process requests resources; if the resources are not available at that time, the process enters a wait state. It may happen that waiting processes will never again change state, because the resources they have requested are held by other waiting processes. This situation is called deadlock. If a process requests an instance of a resource type, the allocation of any instance of the type will satisfy the request. If it will not, then the instances are not identical, and the resource type classes have not been defined properly.

A process must request a resource before using it, and must release the resource after using it. A process may request as many resources as it requires to carry cut its designated task.

Under the normal mode of operation, a process may utilize a resource in only the following sequence:

1. Request: If the request cannot be granted immediately, then the requesting process must wait until it can acquire the resource.
2. Use: The process can operate on the resource.
3. Release: The process releases the resource

5.3. Deadlock Characterization

In deadlock, processes never finish executing and system resources are tied up, preventing other jobs from ever starting.

Necessary Conditions

A deadlock situation can arise if the following four conditions hold simultaneously in a system:

1. Mutual exclusion: At least one resource must be held in a non-sharable mode; that is, only one process at a time can use the resource. If another process requests that resource, the requesting process must be delayed until the resource has been released.
2. Hold and wait: There must exist a process that is holding at least one resource and is waiting to acquire additional resources that are currently being held by other processes.
3. No preemption: Resources cannot be preempted; that is, a resource can be released only voluntarily by the process holding it, after that process, has completed its task.
4. Circular wait: There must exist a set {P0, P1, ..., Pn } of waiting processes such that P0 is waiting for a resource that is held by P1, P1 is waiting for a resource that is held by P2,...., Pn-1 is waiting for a resource that is held by Pn, and Pn is waiting for a resource that is held by P0.

5.3.1. Resource-Allocation Graph

Deadlocks can be described more precisely in terms of a directed graph called a system resource-allocation graph. The set of vertices V is partitioned into two different types of nodes P = {P1, P2,... Pn} the set consisting of all the active processes in the system; and R = {R1, R2,..., R1}, the set consisting of all resource types in the system.

A directed edge from process Pi to resource type Rj is denoted by Pi → Rj, it signifies that process Pi requested an instance of resource type Rj and is currently waiting for that resource. A directed edge from resource type Rjtoprocess Pi is denoted by Rj_ Pi it signifies that an instance of resource type Rj has been allocated to process Pi. A directed edge Pi_ Rj is called a request edge; a directed edgeRj _ Pi is called an assignment edge.

When process Pi requests an instance of resource type Rj, a request edge is inserted in the resource-allocation graph. When this request can be fulfilled, the request edge is instantaneously transformed to an assignment edge. When the process no longer needs access to the, resource it releases the resource, and as a result the assignment edge is deleted.

Definition of a resource-allocation graph, it can be shown that, if the graph contains no cycles, then no process in the system is deadlocked. If, on the other hand, the graph contains the cycle, then a deadlock must exist.

If each resource type has several instances, then a cycle implies that a deadlock has occurred. If the cycle involves only a set of resources types, each of which has only a single instance, then a deadlock has occurred. Each process involved in the cycle is deadlocked. In this case, a cycle in the graph is both a necessary and a sufficient condition for the existence of deadlock.

A set of vertices V and a set of edges E.

- V is partitioned into two types:

  P = {P1, P2, ..., Pn}, the set consisting of all the processes in the system.

  R = {R1, R2, ..., Rm}, the set consisting of all resource types in the system.
- request edge – directed edge P1 Rj
- assignment edge – directed edge RjPi

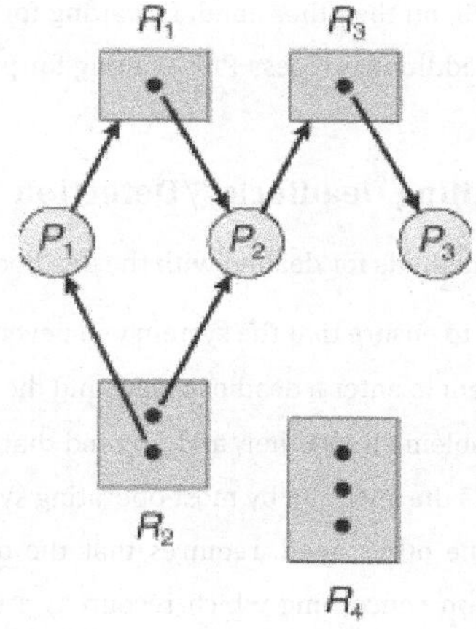

Resource Allocation Graph

If each resource type has several instance, then a cycle does not necessarily imply that a deadlock incurred. In this case, a cycle in the graph is a necessary but not a sufficient condition for the existence of deadlock.

Suppose that process P3requests an instance of resource type R2 Since no resource instance is currently available, a request edge P3 → R2 is added to the graph. At this point, two minimal cycles exist in the system:

P1 → R1 → P2 → R3 → P3 → R2 → P1

P2 → R3 → P3 → R2 → P2

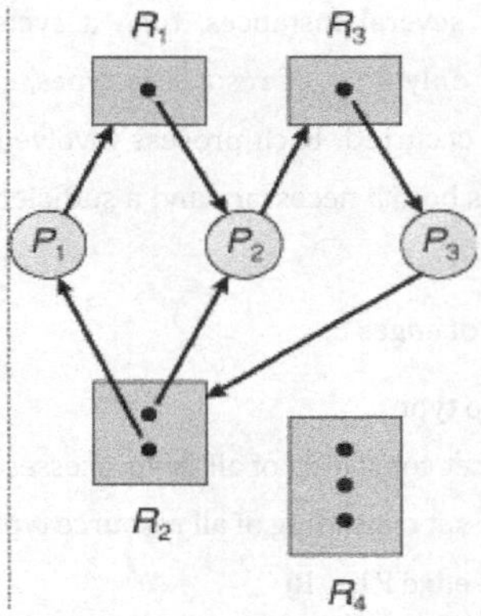

Processes P1, P2, and P3 are deadlocked. Process P2 is waiting for the resource R3, which is held by process P3. Process P3, on the other hand, is waiting for either process P1 or process P2 to release resource R2. In addition, process PI is waiting for process P2 to release resource R1.

5.4. Method For Handling Deadlock //Detection

There are three different methods for dealing with the deadlock problem:

- We can use a protocol to ensure that the system will never enter a deadlock state.
- We can allow the system to enter a deadlock state and then recover.
- We can ignore the problem all together, and pretend that deadlocks never occur in the system. This solution is the one used by most operating systems, including UNIX.

Deadlock avoidance, on the other hand, requires that the operating system be given in advance additional information concerning which resources a process will request and use during its lifetime. With this additional knowledge, we can decide for each request whether or not the process should wait. Each request requires that the system consider the resources currently available, the resources currently allocated to each process, and the future requests and releases of each process, to decide whether the current request can be satisfied or must be delayed.

If a system does not employ either a deadlock-prevention or a deadlock avoidance algorithm, then a deadlock situation may occur If a system does not ensure that a deadlock will never occur, and also does not provide a mechanism for deadlock detection and recovery, then we may arrive at a situation where the system is in a deadlock state yet has no way of recognizing what has happened.

5.5. Deadlock Prevention

For a deadlock to occur, each of the four necessary-conditions must hold. By ensuring that at least on one these conditions cannot hold, we can prevent the occurrence of a deadlock.

5.5.1. Mutual Exclusion

The mutual-exclusion condition must hold for non-sharable resources. For example, a printer cannot be simultaneously shared by several processes. Sharable resources, on the other hand, do not require mutually exclusive access, and thus cannot be involved in a deadlock.

5.5.2. Hold and Wait

1. When whenever a process requests a resource, it does not hold any other resources. One protocol that be used requires each process to request and be allocated all its resources before it begins execution.
2. An alternative protocol allows a process to request resources only when the process has none. A process may request some resources and use them. Before it can request any additional resources, however it must release all the resources that it is currently allocated here are two main disadvantages to these protocols. First, resource utilization may be low, since many of the resources may be allocated but unused for a long period. In the example given, for instance, we can release the tape drive and disk file, and then again request the disk file and printer, only if we can be sure that our data will remain on the disk file. If we cannot be assured that they will, then we must request all resources at the beginning for both protocols. Second, starvation is possible.

5.5.3. No Preemption

If a process that is holding some resources requests another resource that cannot be immediately allocated to it, then all resources currently being held are preempted. That is this resources are implicitly released.

The preempted resources are added to the list of resources for which the process is waiting process will be restarted only when it can regain its old resources, as well as the new ones that it is requesting.

5.5.4. Circular Wait

Circular-wait condition never holds is to impose a total ordering of all resource types, and to require that each process requests resources in an increasing order of enumeration.

Let R = {R1, R2, ..., Rn} be the set of resource types. We assign to each resource type a unique integer number, which allows us to compare two resources and to determine whether one precedes another in our ordering. Formally, we define a one-to-one function F: R _ N, where N is the set of natural numbers.

5.6. Deadlock Avoidance

Prevent deadlocks requests can be made. The restraints ensure that at least one of the necessary conditions for deadlock cannot occur, and, hence, that deadlocks cannot hold. Possible side effects of preventing deadlocks by this, melted, however, are Tow device utilization and reduced system throughput.

An alternative method for avoiding deadlocks is to require additional information about how resources are to be requested.

For example, in a system with one tape drive and one printer, we might be told that process P will request first the tape drive, and later the printer, before releasing both resources.

Process Q on the other hand, will request first the printer, and then the tape drive. With this knowledge of the complete sequence of requests and releases for each process we can decide for each request whether or not the process should wait.

A deadlock-avoidance algorithm dynamically examines the resource-allocation state to ensure that there can never be a circular wait condition. The resource allocation state is defined by the number of available and allocated resources, and the maximum demands of the processes.

5.6.1. Safe State

A state is safe if the system can allocate resources to each process (up to its maximum) in some order and still avoid a deadlock. More formally, a system is ina safe state only if there exists a safe sequence.

A sequence of processes <P1, P2, ..Pn> is a safe sequence for the current allocation state if, for each Pi the resources that Pj can still request can be satisfied by the currently available resources plus the resources held by all the Pj, with j <i. In this situation, if the resources that process Pi needs are not immediately available, then Pi can wait until all Pj have finished. When they have finished, Pi can obtain all of its needed resources, complete its designated task return its allocated resources, and terminate. When Pi terminates, Pi + 1 can obtain its needed resources, and so on.

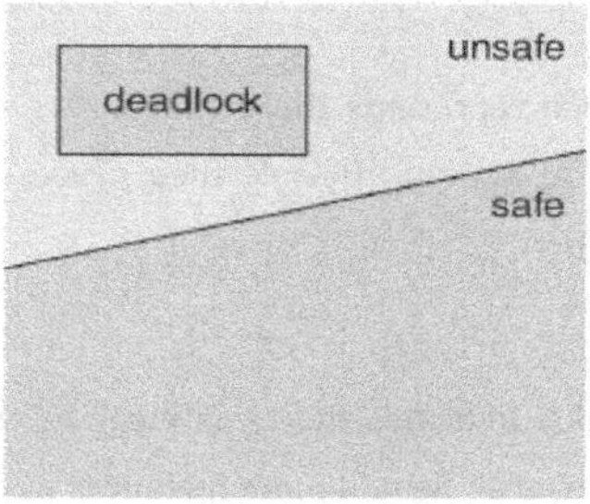

Safe, Unsafe & Deadlock State

If no such sequence exists, then the system state is said to be unsafe.

5.6.2. Resource-Allocation Graph Algorithm

Suppose that process Pi requests resource Rj. The request can be granted only if converting the request edge Pi → Rj to an assignment edge Rj → Pi does not result in the formation of a cycle in the resource-allocation graph.

5.6.3. Banker's Algorithm for Deadlock Avoidance

Banker's algorithm is a deadlock avoidance algorithm. It is named so because this algorithm is used in banking systems to determine whether a loan can be granted or not.

Consider there are n account holders in a bank and the sum of the money in all of their accounts is S. Every time a loan has to be granted by the bank, it subtracts the loan amount from the total money the bank has. Then it checks if that difference is greater than S. It is done because, only then, the bank would have enough money even if all the n account holders draw all their money at once.

Let us assume that there are n processes and m resource types. Some data structures that are used to implement the banker's algorithm are:

1. Available

It is an array of length m. It represents the number of available resources of each type. If Available[j] = k, then there are k instances available, of resource type R(j).

2. Max

It is an n x m matrix which represents the maximum number of instances of each resource that a process can request. If Max[i][j] = k, then the process P(i) can request atmost k instances of resource type R(j).

3. Allocation

It is an n x m matrix which represents the number of resources of each type currently allocated to each process. If Allocation[i][j] = k, then process P(i) is currently allocated k instances of resource type R(j).

4. Need

It is an n x m matrix which indicates the remaining resource needs of each process. If Need[i][j] = k, then process P(i) may need k more instances of resource type R(j) to complete its task.

Data Structures for the Banker's Algorithm

Let *n* = number of processes, and *m* = number of resources types.

n**Available**: Vector of length *m*. If available [*j*] = *k*, there are *k* instances of resource type *Rj* available.

n**Max**: *n x m* matrix. If *Max* [*i,j*] = *k*, then process *Pi* may request at most *k* instances of resour ce type.

*Rj*n**Allocation**: *n* x *m* matrix. If Allocation[*i,j*] = *k* then *Pi* is currently allocated *k* instances of *R j*n**Need**: *n* x *m*

matrix. If *Need*[*i,j*] = *k*, then *Pi* may need *k* more instances of *Rj* to complete its task.

Need [*i,j*] = *Max*[*i,j*] – *Allocation* [*i,j*]

Safety Algorithm

1. Let *Work* and *Finish* be vectors of length *m* and *n*, respectively. Initialize:

Work = *Available*

Finish [*i*] = *false* for *i* = 0, 1, ..., *n*- 1

2. Find and *i* such that both:

(a) *Finish* [*i*] = *false*(b) *Needi £ Work*

If no such *i* exists, go to step 4

3. *Work* = *Work* + *Allocationi*

Finish[*i*] = *true*

go to step 2

4. If *Finish* [*i*] == true for all *i*, then the system is in a safe state

Resource-Request Algorithm for Process Pi

Request = request vector for process *Pi*. If *Requesti* [*j*] = *k* then prccess *Pi* wants *k* instances of resource type *Rj*1.

If *Requesti* £ *Needi* go to step 2. Otherwise, raise error condition, since process has exceeded i ts maximum claim 2.

If *Requesti* £ *Available*, go to step 3. Otherwise *Pi* must wait, since resources are not available 3.

Pretend to allocate requested resources to *Pi* by modifying the state as follows:

Available = *Available* – *Request;*

Allocationi = *Allocationi* + *Requesti*;

Needi = *Needi* – *Requesti;*

l*If safe Þ the resources are allocated to Pi*

l*If unsafe Þ Pi must wait, and the old resource-allocation state is restored*

Example

Total resources in system:

A B C D

6 5 7 6

Available system resources are:

A B C D

3 1 1 2

Processes (currently allocated resources):

A B C D

P1 1 2 2 1

P2 1 0 3 3

P3 1 2 1 0

Processes (maximum resources):

A B C D

P1 3 3 2 2

P2 1 2 3 4

P3 1 3 5 0

Need = maximum resources - currently allocated resources.

Processes (need resources):

A B C D

P1 2 1 0 1

P2 0 2 0 1

P3 0 1 4 0

5.7. Deadlock Detection

If a system does not employ either a deadlock-prevention or a deadlock avoidance algorithm, then a deadlock situation may occur.

- An algorithm that examines the state of the system to determine whether a deadlock has occurred.
- An algorithm to recover from the deadlock.

5.7.1. Single Instance of Each Resource Type

If all resources have only a single instance, then we can define a deadlock detection algorithm that uses a variant of the resource-allocation graph, called a wait-for graph. We obtain this graph from the resource-allocation graph by removing the nodes of type resource and collapsing the appropriate edges.

5.7.2. Several Instances of a Resource Type

The wait-for graph scheme is not applicable to a resource-allocation system with multiple instances of each resource type.

The algorithm used are:

- **Available:** A vector of length m indicates the number of available resources of each type.
- **Allocation:** An n x m matrix defines the number of resources of each type currently allocated to each process.
- **Request:** An n x m matrix indicates the current request of each process. If Request [i, j] = k, then process P, is requesting k more instances of resource type Rj.

5.8. Recovery from Deadlock

When a detection algorithm determines that a deadlock exists, several alternatives exist. One possibility is to inform the operator that a deadlock has spurred, and to let the operator deal with the deadlock manually. The other possibility is to let the system recover from the deadlock automatically. There are two options for breaking a deadlock.

One solution is simply to abort one or more processes to break the circular wait. The second option is to preempt some resources from one or more of the deadlocked processes.

Traditional operating system such as Windows doesn't deal with deadlock recovery as it is time and space consuming process. Real time operating systems use Deadlock recovery.

5.8.1. *Process Termination*

To eliminate deadlocks by aborting a process, we use one of two methods. In both methods, the system reclaims all resources allocated to the terminated processes.

Abort all deadlocked processes: This method clearly will break the dead – lock cycle, but at a great expense, since these processes may have computed for a long time, and the results of these partial computations must be discarded, and probably must be recomputed.

Abort one process at a time until the deadlock cycle is eliminated: This method incurs considerable overhead, since after each process is aborted a deadlock-detection algorithm must be invoked to determine whether a process is still deadlocked.

5.8.2. *Resource Pre-Emption*

To eliminate deadlocks using resource pre-emption, we successively pre-empt some resources from processes and give these resources to other processes until the deadlocks cycle is broken.

The three issues are considered to recover from deadlock

1. Selecting a victim
2. Rollback
3. Starvation

Problems on Deadlock

5.1. Consider a system consisting of 4 resources of same type that are share by 3 processes each of which needs at most two resources. Show that the system is deadlock free.

Ans:

If the system is deadlocked, it implies that each process is holding one resource and is waiting for one more. Since there are 3 processes and 4 resources, one process must be able to obtain two resources. This process requires no more resources and therefore it will return its resources when done.

5.2. Consider a system with m resources of same type being shared by n processes. Resources can be requested and released by processes only on at a time. The system is deadlock free if and only if

a) The sum of all max needs is < m+n

b) The sum of all max needs is > m+n

c) Both of above

d) None

Ans: a

5.3. A proposed solution to the Dining Philosophers deadlock problem is as follows:

```
Philosopher( int i ) {
while(1) {
think();
// grab forks if we can
lock.P()
fork[i].P();
fork[(i+1)%5].P();
lock.V();
eat();
// put down forks
lock.P();
fork[i].V();
fork[(i+1)%5].V();
lock.V();
}
```

There are five philosophers and five forks. All the lock and fork semaphores are initialized to 1.

a) Is the second lock.P/lock.V pair necessary? Why or why not?

b) b. If the second lock.P/lock.V pair isn't necessary, are there any negative consequences to having it there?

Ans:

a) No, it isn't necessary. There is no conflict that can occur doing the V operation, just the P.

b) Yes, there are negative consequences. One innocuous one is that it can cause extra context switches if a philosopher is putting down the forks and has the lock, it will block any philosophers trying to gain access to pick up the forks until both forks are back on.

5.4. Here's a routine used in a multi-threaded process:

```
(void *)some_function( void *arg ) {
if (arg ) {
shared_data1 += 1;
shared_data2 *= shared_data1;
}
else {
cout << "error" << endl;
}
} // some_function
```

The variables shared_data1 and shared_data2 are shared by all the threads in the process. Assume a variable of class Semaphore has been declared, named lock, and is accessible to all the threads.

a) Add operations on lock to ensure mutual exclusion in the critical section of the above function. It is important that the thread be blocked for the minimum time absolutely necessary to ensure the mutual exclusion.

b) What value should lock be initialized to?

Ans:

```
(void *)some_function( void *arg ) {
if (arg ) {
lock.P();
shared_data1 += 1;
shared_data2 *= shared_data1;
lock.V();
}
else {
cout << "error" << endl;
}
} // some_function
```

What value should lock be initialized to? 1

Explanation: We don't need to protect the check of arg as it is local to the routine, nor do we need to protect anything in the else clause, as it accesses no data, so we only need to protect the lines shown. The initial value is 1 to allow exactly one process to initially enter the critical section.

5.5. Three threads need to synchronize their actions so that the following holds:

P1 -> data1 -> P2 -> data2 -> P3 meaning that P1 produces data1, and only when data1 is ready can P2 proceed, etc.

You are guaranteed that each thread will be executed only once, and there are no cycles (ie. what you see above is the whole story).

Here's the skeleton of each thread (note: where it says "do some work" or "do more stuff", it means do work independent of the shared data):

```
thread1() { thread2() { thread3() {
 // do some work //do some work //do some work
   .... ....
   .... ....
   // produce data1 //do stuff with data1 //do stuff with data2
   data1 := 1; //and produce data2 cout << data2 <<endl;
   data2 := data2 * data1;
   //do more stuff //do more stuff // do more stuff
   .... ....    ....
   }}}
```

Add Semaphores and operations on them as needed, assuming that all threads can access them, to ensure the proper order of execution. Indicate the initial value for each Semaphore.

Ans:

```
Sempahore mutex1( 0 ), mutex2( 0 );
thread1() { thread2() { thread3() {
// do some work //do some work //do some work
.... ....
// produce data1 //do stuff with data1 //do stuff with data2
mutex2.P();
data1 := 1; //and produce data2 cout << data2 <<endl;
mutex1.V(); mutex1.P();
data2 := data2 * data1;
mutex2.V();
//do more stuff //do more stuff // do more stuff
.... ....    ....
}}}
```

5.6. A system has four processes P1 through P4 and two resource types R1 and R2. It has 2 units of R1 and 3 units of R2. Given that:

P1 requests 2 units of R2 and 1 unit of R1

P2 holds 2 units of R1 and 1 unit of R2

P3 holds 1 unit of R2

P4 requests 1 unit of R1

Show the resource graph for this state of the system. Is the system in deadlock, and if so, which processes are involved?

Ans:

Here is one complete solution:

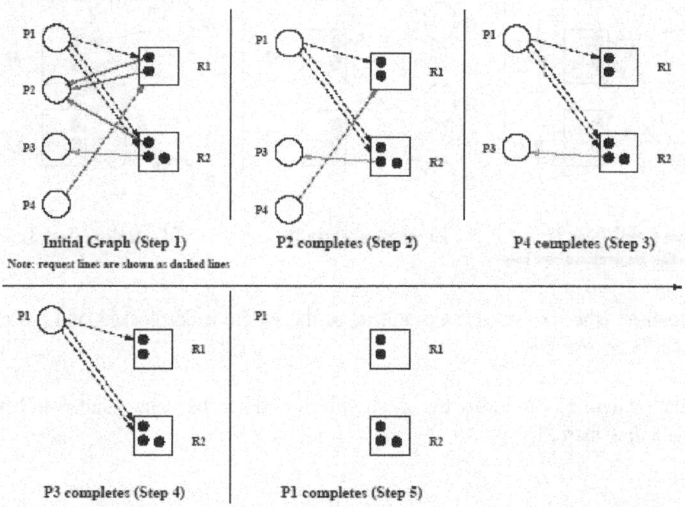

There are many other orders in which things could complete. But one rule is that P2 must complete before P1 completes, as it hold the all the R1 resources and P1 needs one of them.

5.7. A system has five processes P1 through P5 and four resource types R1 through R4.

There are 2 units of each resource type. Given that:

P1 holds 1 unit of R1 and requests 1 unit of R4

P2 holds 1 unit of R3 and requests 1 unit of R2

P3 holds one unit of R2 and requests 1 unit of R3

P4 requests 1 unit of R4

P5 holds one unit of R3 and 1 unit of R2, and requests 1 unit of R3

Show the resource graph for this state of the system. Is the system in deadlock, and if so, which processes are involved?

Ans:

Here is one complete solution:

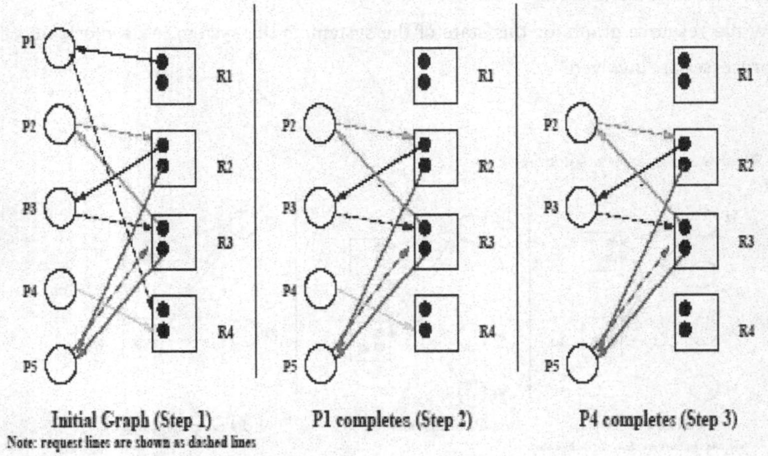

At this point no other processes can complete, so the system is deadlocked, and process P2, P3, and P5 are involved.

An alternate ordering of reducing the graph, which leads ot the same result is to have P4 complete first, then P1.

5.8. Given 5 total units of the resource, tell whether the following system is in a safe or unsafe state.

Process	Used	Max
P1	1	2
P2	1	3
P3	2	4
P4	0	5

The system is in a safe state. Here's why. You have 1 unit left. If you give it to P1, it can complete and release the two units. Then P2 and P3 can complete in either order. When P3 is done, it frees up enough resources for P4 to complete.

5.9. Given a total of 5 units of resource type 1 and 4 units of resource type 2, tell whether the following system is in a safe or unsafe state. Show your work.

	Type 1		Type 2	
Process	Used	Max	Used	Max
P1	1	2	1	3
P2	1	3	1	2
P3	2	4	1	4

Ans:

The system is in an unsafe state. In order to be sure a process can complete, it will need its request of all resource types to be satisfied, so you need to look at the need for each process for all resource types and see if what is available can satisfy any process's needs.

In this example we have the following needs:

Process	Type 1	Type 2
P1	1	2
P2	2	1
P3	2	3

As we have only 1 unit of each resource type available, and no process has a need that can be satisfied, so the system is unsafe.

5.10. Given a total of 10 units of a resource type, and given the safe state shown below, should process 2 be granted a request of 2 additional resources? Show your work.

Process	Used	Max
P1	2	5
P2	1	6
P3	2	6
P4	1	2
P5	1	4

Ans:

The system is in an unsafe state. If we give the 2 units to P2, we would have the following needs:

Process	Need
P1	3
P2	3
P3	4
P4	1
P5	3

We have 1 unit left, which we can give to P4, which will release only 2 units of the processes remaining, no process can complete with only 2 units, so the system is unsafe.

5.11. Given a total of 10 units of a resource type, and given the safe state shown below, should process 2 be granted a request of 2 additional resources? Show your work.

Process	Used	Max
P1	2	5
P2	1	6
P3	2	6
P4	1	2
P5	1	4

Ans:

The system is in an unsafe state. If we give the 2 units to P2, we would have the following needs:

Process	Need
P1	3
P2	3
P3	4
P4	1
P5	3

We have 1 unit left, which we can give to P4, which will release only 2 units of the processes remaining, no process can complete with only 2 units, so the system is unsafe.

5.12. List three examples of deadlocks that are not related to a computer- system environment.

Ans:

- Two cars crossing a single-lane bridge from opposite directions.
- A person going down a ladder while another person is climbing up the ladder.
- Two trains traveling toward each other on the same track.

5.13. Consider a system consisting of four resources of the same type that are shared by three processes, each of which needs at most two resources. Show that the system is deadlockfree.

Ans:

Suppose the system is deadlocked. This implies that each process is holding one resource and is waiting for one more. Since there are three processes and four resources, one process must be able to obtain two resources. This process requires no more resources and, therefore it will return its resources when done.

5.14. When a process is rolled out of memory, it loses its ability to use the CPU (at least for a while). Describe another situation where a process loses its ability to use the CPU, but where the process does not get rolled out.

a) When an interrupt occurs.

b) When thrashing occurs.

c) When deadlock occurs.

d) While swapping.

Ans: a

5.9. Goals of Protection

Protection can improve reliability by detecting latent errors at the interfaces between component subsystems. Early detection of interface errors can often prevent contamination of a healthy subsystem by a malfunctioning subsystem. Also, an unprotected resource cannot defend against use by an unauthorized or incompetent user. A protection oriented system provides means to distinguish between authorized and unauthorized usage.

The role of protection in a computer system is to provide a mechanism for the enforcement of the policies governing resource use.

These policies can be established in a variety of ways. Some are fixed in the design of the system, while others are formulated by the management of a system. Still others are defined by the individual users to protect their own files and programs. A protection system must have the flexibility to enforce a variety of policies. The application programmer needs to use protection mechanism.

5.10. Principles of Protection

- Frequently, a guiding principle can be used throughout a project, such as the design of an operating system. Following this principle simplifies design decisions and keeps the system consistent and easy to understand. A key, time tested guiding principle for protection is the principle of least privilege. It dictates that programs, users, and even systems be given just enough privileges to perform their tasks.
- An operating system following the principle of least privilege implements its features, programs, system calls, and data structures so that failure or compromise of a component does the minimum damage and allows the minimum damage to be done.
- The principle of least privilege can help produce a more secure computing environment.

5.11. Domain of Protection

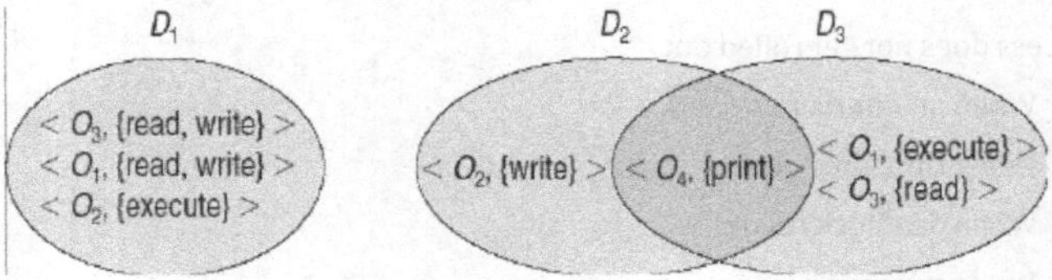

- A computer system is a collection of processes and objects. By objects, we mean both hardware objects (such as the CPU, memory segments, printers, disks, tape drives), and software objects (such as files, programs, and semaphore).
- Protection domain is process that operates within a protection domain, which specifies the resources that the process may access. Each domain defines a set of objects and .the types of operations that may be invoked on each object.
- The ability to execute an operation on an object is an access right. A domain is a collection of access ' rights, each of which is an ordered pair <object-name, rights-set>. For example, if domain D has the access right <file F, {read, write}>, then a process executing in domain D can both read and write file F, if cannot, however, perform any other operation on that object.
  1. Each user may be a domain. The set of objects that can be accessed depends on the identity of the user. Domain switching occur when the user is changed — generally when one user logs out and another user logs in.
  2. Each process may be a domain. In this case, the set of objects that can be accessed depends on the identity of the process. Domain switching corresponds to one process sending a message to another process, and then waiting for a response.
  3. Each procedure may be a domain. In this case, the set of objects that can be accessed corresponds to the local variables define Domain switching occurs when a procedure call is made.

5.12. Access Matrix

- Our model of protection can be viewed abstractly as a matrix, called an access matrix. The rows of the access matrix represent domains, and the columns represent objects. Each entry in the matrix consists of a set of access rights.
- Because objects are defined explicitly by the column, we can omit the object name from the access right. The entry access (i, j) defines the set of operations that a process, executing in domain Di, can invoke on object Oj.

- We consider the access matrix shown in Figure. There are four domains and four objects: three files (F1, F2, F3), and one laser printer. When a process executes in domain D1, it can read files F1 and F3.. A process executing in domain D4 has the same privileges as it does in domain D1, but in addition, it can also write onto files F1 and F3. Note that the laser printer can be accessed only by a process executing in domain D2.
- The access-matrix scheme provides us with the mechanism for specifying a variety of policies. More specifically, we must ensure that a process executing in domain Di can access only those objects specified in row i, and then only as allowed by the access matrix entries.
- Policy decisions concerning protection can be implemented by the access matrix. The users normally decide the contents of the access-matrix entries.
- Allowing controlled change to the contents of the access-matrix entries requires three additional operations: copy, owner, and control.

Object Domain	F1	F2	F3	printer
D1	Read		Read	
D2				Print
D3		read	Execute	
D4	Read write		Read write	

Access Matrix

5.13. Revocation of Access Rights

In a dynamic protection system, we may sometimes need to revolve access rights to objects shared by different users. Various questions about revocation may arise:

- **Immediate versus delayed:** Does revocation occur immediately, or is it delayed? If revocation is delayed, can we find out when it will take place?
- **Selective versus general:** When an access right to an object revoked, does it affect all the users who have an access right to that object, or can we specify a select group of users whose access rights should be revoked?
- **Partial versus total:** Can a subset of the rights associated with an object be revoked, or must we revoke all access rights for this object?

- **Temporary versus permanent:** Can access be revoked permanently (that is, the revoked access right will never again be available), or can access be revoked and later be obtained again?

Schemes that implements revocation for capabilities include the following:

- **Reacquisition:** Periodically, capabilities are deleted from each domain. If a process wants to use a capability, it may find that capability has been deleted. The process may then try to reacquire the capability. If access has been revoked, the process will not be able to reacquire the capability.
- **Back pointers:** A list of pointers is maintained with each object, pointing to all capabilities associated with that object. When revocation is required, we can follow this pointers, changing the capabilities as necessary. This scheme was adopted in the MULTICS system.
- **Indirection:** The capabilities point indirectly, not directly, to the objects. Each capability points to a unique entry in a global trade, which in turn points to the object. We implement revocation by searching the global table for the desired entry and deleting it. It does not allow selective revocation.
- **Keys:** A key is a unique bit pattern that can be associated with a capability. This key is defined when the capability is created, and it can be neither modifier\ed nor inspected by the process that owns the capability. A master key is associated with each object; it can be defined or replaced with the set-key operation.

Capability-based Systems

- The goal of a single operating system mechanism capable of supporting a wide range of security policies is not a new goal. The Hydra operating system developed in the 1970's separated its access control mechanisms from the definition of its security policy. Hydra was a capability-based system, although the developers of the system recognized the limitations of a simple capability model and introduced several enhancements to the basic capability mechanisms. The Hydra approach was taken even further by the KeyKOS and EROS systems. Though popular, capability mechanisms are poorly suited to providing policy flexibility, because they allow the holder of a capability to control the direct propagation of that capability, whereas a critical requirement for supporting security policies is the ability to control the propagation of access rights in accordance with the policy. The enhancements introduced by Hydra and KeyKOS are intended to limit such propagation, but the resulting systems still generally only support the specific policies they were designed to satisfy, at the cost of significant complexity that diminishes the attraction of the capability model in the first place.

- Primarily with an interest in solving the problem of supporting a multilevel security policy within a capability-based system, a few capability-based systems (*e.g.*, SCAP, ICAP, Trusted Mach introduced mechanisms that validated every propagation or use of a capability against the security policy. Kain and Landwehr developed a taxonomy to characterize such systems. In these systems, the simplicity of the capability mechanism is retained, but capabilities serve only as a least privilege mechanism rather than a mechanism for recording and propagating the security policy. This is a potentially valuable use of capabilities. However, the designs for these systems do not define the mechanisms by which the security policy is queried to validate capabilities, and those mechanisms are essential to providing policy flexibility. The Flask architecture described in this paper could be employed to provide the security decisions needed to validate the capabilities in these systems. In the Flask prototype, the architecture is used in exactly this way.

5.14. Summary

A deadlocked state occurs when two or more processes are waiting indefinitely for an event that can be caused only one of the waiting processes.

There are three principal methods for dealing with deadlocks:

Use some protocol to prevent or avoid deadlocks, entering that the system will never enter a deadlocked state.

Allow the system to enter a deadlocked state, detect it, and then recover.

Ignore the problem altogether and pretend that deadlocks never occur in the system.

Deadlock prevention is a set of methods for ensuring that at least one of the necessary conditions cannot hold. Deadlock avoidance requires additional information about how resources are to be requested. Deadlock avoidance algorithm dynamically examines the resource allocation state to ensure that a circular wait condition can never exist. Deadlock occur only when some process makes a request that cannot be granted immediately.

Computer system contains many objects, and they need to be protected from misuse. Objects may be hardware (such as memory, CPU time, and I/O devices) or software(such as files, programs, and semaphores). An access right is permission to perform an operation on an object. A domain is a set of access rights. Processes execute in domains and may use any of the access rights in the domain to access and manipulate objects. During its lifetime, a process may be either bound to a protection domain or allowed to switch from one domain to another.

The access matrix is a general model of protection that provides a mechanism for protection without imposing a particular protection policy on the system or its users. The separation of policy and mechanism is an important design policy.

Real systems are much more limited than the general model and tend to provide protection for files.

5.15. Model Question

1. Write a short note on deadlock?
2. Explain the characteristic of deadlock?
3. Describe various methods for deadlock prevention?
4. Explain the resource allocation graph?
5. Write a note on safe state'?
6. Explain how deadlocks are detected and corrected?
7. What are the difference between a deadlock prevention and deadlock Avoidance?
8. Define and explain Access matrix?
9. How does the systems that implement the principle of least privilege still have protection systems?
10. Discuss strengths and weaknesses of implementing an access matrix using access list?
11. Explain Domain Structure?

5.16. Objective Questions

1. The systems which allows only one process execution at a time, are called.

   a) Uniprogramming systems

   b) Uniprocessing systems

   c) Unitasking systems

   d) None of the mentioned

2. In operating system, each process has its own.

   a) Address space and global variables

   b) Open files

   c) Pending alarms, signals and signal handlers

   d) All of the mentioned

3. In Unix, Which system call creates the new process?

a) fork

b) create

c) new

d) None of the mentioned

4. A process can be terminated due to,

a) Normal exit

b) Fatal error

c) Killed by another process

d) All of the mentioned

5. What is the ready state of a process?

a) When process is scheduled to run after some execution

b) When process is unable to run until some task has been completed

c) When process is using the CPU

d) None of the mentioned

6. What is inter-process communication?

a) Communication within the process

b) Communication between two process

c) Communication between two threads of same process

d) None of the mentioned

7. A set of processes is deadlock if,

a) Each process is blocked and will remain so forever

b) Each process is terminated

c) All processes are trying to kill each other

d) None of the mentioned

8. A process stack does not contain,

a) Function parameters

b) Local variables

c) Return addresses

d) PID of child process

9. Which system call returns the process identifier of a terminated child?

a) wait

b) exit

c) fork

d) get

Protection

1. Which principle states that programs, users and even the systems be given just enough privileges to perform their task?

   a) Principle of operating system

   b) Principle of least privilege

   c) Principle of process scheduling

   d) None of the mentioned

2. ______ is an approach to restricting system access to authorized users.

   a) Role-based access control

   b) Process-based access control

   c) Job-based access control

   d) None of the mentioned

3. The protection domain of a process contains,

   a) Object name

   b) Rights-set

   c) Both object name and rights-set

   d) None of the mentioned

4. For system protection, a process should access.

   a) All the resources

   b) **Only those resources for which it has authorization**

   c) Few resources but authorization is not required

   d) All of the mentioned

5. Access matrix model for user authentication contains,

   a) A list of objects

   b) A list of domains

   c) A function which returns an object's type

   d) All of the mentioned

6. If the set of resources available to the process is fixed throughout the process's lifetime then its domain is,

   a) Static

   b) Dynamic

   c) Neither static nor dynamic

   d) None of the mentioned

7. Global table implementation of matrix table contains,

    a) Domain

    b) Object

    c) Right-set

    d) All of the mentioned

8. Which one of the following is capability based protection system?

    a) Hydra

    b) Cambridge CAP system

    c) Both hydra and cambridge CAP system

    d) None of the mentioned

9. In UNIX, domain switch is accomplished via,

    a) File system

    b) User

    c) Superuser

    d) None of the mentioned

10. For a domain _____ is a list of objects together with the operation allowed on these objects.

    a) Capability list

    b) Access list

    c) Both capability and access list

    d) None of the mentioned

Code No: RT31055

R13 SET - 1

III B. TECH I SEMESTER SUPPLEMENTARY EXAMINATIONS, MAY -2016

OPERATING SYSTEMS

(COMMON TO CSE AND IT)

TIME: 3 HOURS MAX **MARKS: 70**

Note: 1. Question Paper consists of two parts **(Part-A and Part-B)**

2. Answering the question in **Part-A** is compulsory

3. Answer any **THREE** Questions from **Part-B**

******

Part –A

1. a) Write short notes on device controller and driver. [3M]

b) What is a Dispatcher? Mention its functions. [4M]

c) Describe how the Swap () instruction can be used to provide mutual exclusion that satisfies the bounded-waiting requirement. [4M]

d) Explain the difference between internal and external fragmentation. [4M]

e) What are the various data structures used for implementing banker's algorithm? Provide a brief description of each. [4M]

f) Write short notes on virtual file system. [3M]

Part -B

2. a) Write an overview of computer system. [10M]

b) Describe the features of a distributed operating system. [6M]

3. a) What is a scheduler? List and describe different types of schedulers. [6M]

b) Write in detail about the thread libraries. [10M]

4. a) Present producer-consumer problem. Explain how to solve it. [8M]

b) Distinguish between counting and binary semaphores. Show when does the semaphore definition requires busy waiting. Suggest a solution to overcome this problem. [8M]

5. a) Consider the reference string: 7, 0, 1, 2, 0, 3, 0, 4, 2, 3, 0, 3, 2, 1, 2, 0, 1, 7, 0, 1 for a memory with three frames. Trace FIFO, optimal, and LRU page replacement algorithms. [6M]

b) Discuss in detail about various page table structures. [10M]

6. a) Explain in detail about deadlock detection techniques. [8M]

b) Explain how to recover the system from a deadlock. [8M]

7. a) How to provide protection to a file system? Explain. [8M]

b) Write in detail about the on-disk and in-memory structures used to implement a file system. [8M]

****

Code No: RT31055 R13 SET – 1

III B. Tech I Semester Supplementary Examinations, May- 2018

Operating Systems

(Common to Computer Science Engineering and Information Technology)

Time: 3 hours Max **Marks: 70**

Note: 1. Question Paper consists of two parts **(Part-A and Part-B)**

2. Answering the question in **Part-A** is compulsory

3. Answer any **THREE** Questions from **Part-B**

******

Part –A

1. a) Differentiate between kernel mode and user mode. [3M]

b) Define multi-threading? Explain its benefits. [4M]

c) What is a critical section? Give examples. [4M]

d) What do you mean by page fault? [4M]

e) What are the necessary conditions for deadlock? [4M]

f) Compare bit map based allocation of blocks on the disk with a free block list. [3M]

Part -B

2. a) Explain the purpose of system calls and discuss the system calls related to process control and communication in brief. [8M]

b) Explain evolution of operating systems. [8M]

3. a) Describe the differences among long-term scheduling. short-term, and medium- term scheduling. [8M]

b) What are the components of process control block? Explain. [8M]

4. a) Write Peterson Algorithm for 2-process synchronization to critical section problem and discuss briefly. [8M]

   b) What are the semaphores? How do they implement mutual exclusion? [8M]

5. Consider the following page reference string: 1, 2, 3, 4, 2, 1, 5, 6, 1, 2, 3, 7, 6, 3, 2, 1, 2, 3, 6. How many page faults would occur for the LRU,FIFO,LFU and optimal page replacement algorithms assuming two and five frames? [16M]

6. a) How can a system recover from a deadlock? Explain. [8M]

   b) Explain the Resource-Allocation Graph Algorithm for deadlock prevention. [8M]

7. a) Explain the different file access methods in detail. [8M]

   b) Describe any two disk scheduling algorithms with suitable illustrations. [8M]

******

Code No: RT31055 R13 SET - 1

III B. Tech I Semester Regular/Supplementary Examinations, October/November - 2016

Operating Systems

(Common to CSE and IT)

Time: 3 hours **Max. Marks: 70**

Note: 1. Question Paper Consists of Two Parts **(Part-A and Part-B)**

2. Answering the Question in **Part-A** is Compulsory

3. Answer Any **THREE** Questions From **Part-B**

****

Part A

1. a) Describe the typical elements of the process control block. [3M]

   b) Define System Call? List out any four Process Control System Calls. [4M]

   c) Distinguish between counting and binary semaphores. [4M]

   d) What is the purpose of paging the page tables? [4M]

   e) Discuss the Safe, unsafe, and deadlock state spaces. [3M]

   f) What is a File? Describe the attributes of a file. [4M]

Part B

2. a) Explain the Time-shared operating system. [4M]

   b) Discuss the Simple Operating System Structure. Describe the layers of the Kernel. [8M]

   c) Explain the difference between micro-kernel and macro-kernel. [4M]

3. a) Compare and contrast thread and process. [3M]

   b) Define Process. Explain various steps involved in change of a process state with process state neat transition diagram. [8M]

   c) Discuss Multithreading Models with neat diagrams. [5M]

4. a) What is a Critical Section? Discuss the solution of the Critical Section problem.[8M]

b) Explain in detail Readers and Writers Problem of Synchronization. [8M]

5. a) Discuss the procedure for handling the page fault in demand paging. [8M]

   b) Illustrate the page-replacement algorithms i) FIFO ii) Optimal Page Replacement use the reference string 7, 0,1, 2, 0, 3, 0, 4, 2, 3, 0, 3, 2,1, 2, 0, 1, 7, 0,1 for a memory with three frames. [8M]

6. a) How to Recover From Deadlock situations? Discuss in detail. [8M]

   b) Explain deadlock avoidance process using Resource-Allocation-Graph. [8M]

7. a) Write short notes on: i) FCFS and ii) SSTF Disk Scheduling schemes. [8M]

   b) Discuss the Indexed File allocation method with an example. [8M]

******

Code No: RT31055 R13 SET - 2

III B. Tech I Semester Regular/Supplementary Examinations, October/November - 2016

Operating Systems

(Common to CSE and IT)

Time: 3 hours **Max. Marks: 70**

Note: 1. Question Paper Consists of Two Parts **(Part-A and Part-B)**

2. Answering the Question in **Part-A** is Compulsory

3. Answer any **THREE** Questions From **Part-B**

******

Part –A

1. a) Draw MS-DOS Operating System structure. [3M]

   b) Describe different attributes of the process. [4M]

   c) Define Busy Waiting? How to overcome busy waiting using Semaphore operations. [4M]

   d) Why segmentation and paging are sometimes combined into one scheme? [4M]

   e) Discuss the usage of wait-for graph scheme. [3M]

   f) Explain the information associated with an open file. [4M]

Part -B

2. a) Discuss UNIX Operating system structure. [4M]

   b) Explain different categories of System calls with suitable examples. [8M]

   c) Define Multitasking. Discuss the Timeshared operating System. [4M]

3. a) Differences between preemptive scheduling and non preemptive Scheduling. [3M]

   b) What is IPC? Explain in detail the inter process communication models [8M]

   c) Describe the differences among short-term, medium-term, and long term Schedulers. [5]

4. a) What is Peterson's Solution? Discuss the Critical Section problem using Peterson's Solution. [8M]

   b) Explain in detail Synchronization implementation in Linux. [8M]

5. a) What is demand paging? Discuss the hardware support required to support demand paging. [8M]

   b) Illustrate the page-replacement algorithms i) LRU ii) LRU-Approximation Page Replacement use the reference string 7, 0,1, 2, 0, 3, 0, 4, 2, 3, 0, 3, 2,1, 2, 0, 1, 7, 0,1 for a memory with three frames [8M]

6. a) Discuss deadlock avoidance using banker's algorithm with suitable example. [8M]

   b) Explain Deadlock Detection scheme for Several Instances of a resource Type. [8M]

7. a) Explain various file access methods with suitable examples. [8M]

   b) Discuss the Schematic view of a virtual file system with neat sketch. [8M]

*****

Code No: RT31055 R13 SET - 3

III B. Tech I Semester Regular/Supplementary Examinations, October/November - 2016

Operating Systems

(Common to CSE and IT)

Time: 3 hours **Max. Marks: 70**

Note: 1. Question Paper Consists of Two Parts **(Part-A and Part-B)**

2. Answering the Question in **Part-A** is Compulsory

3. Answer Any **THREE** Questions From **Part-B**

******

Part –A

1. a) What are Operating-System Services? [3M]

b) Describe the benefits of multithreaded programming. [4M]

c) Describe disadvantages of the semaphore. [4M]

d) Explain why sharing a reentrant module is easier, when segmentation is used than when pure paging is used. [4M]

e) Describe the Methods for Handling Deadlocks. [3M]

f) Discuss UNIX File System Mounting. [4M]

Part -B

2. a) Explain the overview of an Operating system with neat sketch. [4M]

b) Describe essential properties of Real Time and Network operating Systems [8M]

c) Explain models of distributed systems. [4M]

3. a) What is a Scheduler? Describe different CPU Schedulers. [5M]

b) Define starvation. Which of the scheduling algorithms result in starvation? Explain. [6M]

c) Describe the actions taken by a kernel to context-switch between processes [5M]

4. a) Define atomic instruction. Explain with an example. [4M]

b) Explain wait and signal semaphore operations without busy waiting. [4M]

c) Give a solution for second Readers-Writers problem. [8M]

5. a) Explain implementation of virtual memory through Demand Paging. [8M]

   b) Discuss the Hierarchical Paging structure. [8M]

6. a) Discuss deadlock avoidance using Resource-Allocation-Graph Algorithm. [8M]

   b) Explain Deadlock detection algorithm with an example. [8M]

7. a) Explain different operations on File. [8M]

   b) Write short notes on :i) Contiguous and ii) Linked File allocation methods [8M]

*****

Code No: RT31055 R13 SET - 4

III B. TECH I SEMESTER REGULAR/SUPPLEMENTARY EXAMINATIONS, OCTOBER/NOVEMBER - 2016

OPERATING SYSTEMS

(COMMON TO CSE AND IT)

TIME: 3 HOURS **MAX. MARKS: 70**

Note: 1. Question Paper Consists of Two Parts **(Part-A and Part-B)**

2. Answering the Question in **Part-A** is Compulsory

3. Answer any **THREE** Questions from **Part-B**

******

Part –A

1. a) Describe the Operating-System Operations. [3M]

b) Define Cooperating process? What is the environment need in Cooperating processes? [4M]

c) What is a Monitor? Give the schematic view of the basic monitor. [4M]

d) Write short note on demand paging. [4M]

e) What is the usage of Resource-Allocation Graph? [4M]

f) Define the terms seek time & rotational latency. [3M]

Part -B

2. a) What is an Operating system? Describe the Operating-System Functions. [4M]

b) Explain briefly Layered Operating system structure with neat sketch . [8M]

c) Differentiate protection and security. [4M]

3. a) Explain Inter Process Communication models in detail. [8M]

b) What are the differences between user-level threads and kernel-level threads? [4M]

c) Explain allocation and de allocation of resources when a process is created & terminated respectively in UNIX. [4M]

4. a) Give a solution to Readers-Writers problem using Monitors. [8M]

b) Define semaphore? Explain the usage and implementation of semaphores. [8M]

5. a) What is the cause of thrashing? How does the system detect thrashing?

   How to eliminate this problem? [8M]

   b) What is Paging? Discuss the Paging model of logical and physical memory. [8M]

6. a) What is a deadlock? Consider the deadlock situation that could occur in the din in philosopher's problem when the philosophers obtain the chopsticks one at a time. [8M]

   Discuss how the four necessary conditions for deadlock indeed hold in this setting.

   What are the solutions for this problem?

   b) Explain recovery from deadlock after detection. [8M]

7. a) Discuss various types of disk storage attachments. [8M]

   b) Explain File Free Space management approaches. [8M]

*****

Code No: RT31055 R13 SET - 1

III B. TECH I SEMESTER REGULAR EXAMINATIONS, NOVEMBER - 2015

OPERATING SYSTEMS

(COMMON TO CSE AND IT)

TIME: 3 HOURS **MAX. MARKS: 70**

Note: 1. Question Paper consists of two parts **(Part-A and Part-B)**

2. Answering the question in **Part-A** is compulsory

3. Answer any **THREE** Questions from **Part-B**

*****

Part A

1. a) Define Operating System. List the objectives of an operating system. [3M]

   b) With a neat diagram, explain various states of a process. [4M]

   c) Give the Peterson's solution to the Critical section problem. [4M]

   d) Distinguish between Logical and Physical address space. [3M]

   e) What are the necessary conditions for the occurrence of deadlock? [4M]

   f) What are the various attributes that are associated with an opened file? [4M]

Part B

2. a) With a neat diagram, explain the layered structure of UNIX operating system. [8M]

   b) What are the advantages and disadvantages of using the same system call interface for manipulating both files and devices? [8M]

3. a) What is a process? Explain about various fields of Process Control Block. [8M]

   b) What are the advantages of inter-process communication? How communication takes place in a shared-memory environment? Explain. [8M]

4. a) What is a Critical Section problem? Give the conditions that a solution to the critical section problem must satisfy. [8M]

   b) What is Dining Philosophers problem? Discuss the solution to Dining philosopher's problem using monitors. [8M]

5. a) What is a Virtual Memory? Discuss the benefits of virtual memory technique. [8M]

b) What is Thrashing? What is the cause of Thrashing? How does the system detect Thrashing? What can the system do to eliminate this problem? [8M]

6. a) What is a deadlock? How deadlocks are detected? [8M]

   b) Explain the Resource-Allocation-Graph algorithm for deadlock avoidance. [8M]

7. a) Briefly explain about single-level, two-level and Tree-Structured directories. [8M]

   b) Explain and compare the SCAN and C-SCAN disk scheduling algorithms. [8M]

Code No: RT31055

R13

SET - 2

III B. TECH I SEMESTER REGULAR EXAMINATIONS, NOVEMBER- 2015

OPERATING SYSTEMS

(COMMON TO CSE AND IT)

TIME: 3 HOURS **MAX. MARKS: 70**

Note: 1. Question Paper Consists of Two Parts **(Part-A and Part-B)**

2. Answering the Question in **Part-A** is compulsory

3. Answer Any **THREE** Questions From **Part-B**

*****

Part A

1. a) Explain how multiprogramming increases the utilization of CPU. [3M]

b) What are the advantages of inter-process communication? Also explain various implementations of inter-process communication. [4M]

c) What is a Semaphore? Also give the operations for accessing semaphores. [4M]

d) What is the purpose of Paging and Page tables? [3M]

e) What are the various methods for handling deadlocks? [4M]

f) Briefly explain the indexed allocation method. [4M]

Part B

2. a) Explain the Dual-Mode operation of an operating system. [8M]

b) Mention the objectives and functions of Real-Time Embedded systems. [8M]

3. a) With a neat sketch, explain the process state diagram. [8M]

b) What are the criteria for evaluating the CPU scheduling algorithms? Why do we need it? [8M]

4. a) What is a semaphore? List the types of semaphores and Show that, if the wait () and signal () semaphore operations are not executed atomically, then mutual exclusion may be violated. [10M]

b) Discuss the Bounded-Buffer problem. [6M]

5. a) What is a page fault? Explain the steps involved in handling a page fault with a neat sketch. [8M]

   b) Consider the following page reference string:

   1,2,3,4,2,1,5,6,2,1,2,3,7,6,3,2,1,2,3,6

   How many page faults would occur for the optimal page replacement algorithm, assuming three frames and all frames are initially empty. [8M]

6. a) Write about deadlock conditions and bankers algorithm in detail. [10M]

   b) Discuss various techniques to recover from the deadlock. [6M]

7. a) Write in detail about file attributes, operations and types and structures. [8M]

   b) Explain in detail about various ways of accessing disk storage. [8M]

Code No: RT31055 R13 SET - 3

III B. TECH I SEMESTER REGULAR EXAMINATIONS, NOVEMBER- 2015

OPERATING SYSTEMS

(COMMON TO CSE AND IT)

TIME: 3 HOURS **MAX. MARKS: 70**

Note: 1. Question Paper Consists of Two Parts **(Part-A and Part-B)**

2. Answering the Question in **Part-A** is Compulsory

3. Answer Any THREE Questions From **Part-B**

*****

Part A

1. a) What are the various security issues that arise in multiprogramming and time shared systems? [3M]

b) Describe the differences among short-term, medium-term, and long-term scheduling. [4M]

c) Briefly explain the Readers-Writers problem. [4M]

d) What are the disadvantages of single contiguous memory allocation? [3M]

e) Explain the various ways of aborting a process in order to eliminate deadlocks. [4M]

f) What is the drawback of Network-attached storage systems? [4M]

Part B

2. a) With a neat sketch, describe the services that an operating system provides to users, processes and other systems. [8M]

b) Distinguish between client-server and peer-to-peer models of distributed systems. [8M]

3. a) Define a Thread? Give the benefits of multithreading. What resources are used when a thread is created? How do they differ from those used when a process is created? [8M]

b) Explain the Round Robin scheduling algorithm with a suitable example. [8M]

4. a) State the Critical Section problem. Illustrate the software based solution to the Critical Section problem. [8M]

b) How does the signal () operation associated with monitors differ from the corresponding operation defined for semaphores. [8M]

5. a) What are the disadvantages of single contiguous memory allocation? Explain. [6M]

   b) Discuss the hardware support required to support demand paging. [10M]

6. a) How does deadlock avoidance differ from deadlock prevention? Write about deadlock avoidance algorithm in detail. [10M]

   b) Is it possible to have a deadlock involving only a single process? Explain. [6M]

7. a) Explain the various methods for free-space management. [10M]

   b) Discuss various issues involved in selecting appropriate disk scheduling algorithm. [6M]

Code No: RT31055 R13 SET - 4

III B. Tech I Semester Regular Examinations, November- 2015

OPERATING SYSTEMS

(Common to CSE and IT)

Time: 3 hours **Max. Marks: 70**

Note: 1. Question Paper Consists of Two Parts **(Part-A and Part-B)**

2. Answering the Question in **Part-A** is Compulsory

3. Answer Any **THREE** Questions From **Part-B**

*****

Part A

1. a) Explain the importance of Real-Time Embedded systems. [3M]

   b) Define Thread. Write the differences between user-level and kernel-level threads. [4M]

   c) Define Monitor. Explain how it overcomes the drawback of semaphores. [4M]

   d) Explain how demand paging affects the performance of a computer system. [4M]

   e) Write about Resource-Allocation graph. [4M]

   f) Explain the bit vector representation of free space management. [3M]

Part B

2. a) What is a System call? Explain the various types of system calls provided by an operating system. [8M]

   b) What is the purpose of interrupts? What are the differences between a trap and an interrupt? Can traps be generated by a user program? Explain the purpose with an example. [8M]

3. a) Distinguish between preemptive and non-preemptive scheduling. Explain each type with an example. [8M]

   b) Describe the actions taken by a thread library to context-switch between user- level threads. [8M]

4. a) What is synchronization? Explain how semaphores can be used to deal with n- process critical section problem. [8M]

b) Discuss Mutual-exclusion implementation with test and set () instruction. [8M]

5. a) Explain the difference between External fragmentation and Internal fragmentation. How to solve the fragmentation problem using paging. [8M]

   b) Discuss various issued related to the allocation of frames to processes. [8M]

6. a) Discuss the necessary conditions that cause deadlock situation to occur. [8M]

   b) Discuss various methods for the prevention of deadlocks. [8M]

7. a) Explain the Indexed allocation of disk space. [8M]

   b) Explain and compare the FCFS and SSTF disk scheduling algorithms. [8M]

Code No: RT31055 R13 SET - 1

III B. Tech I Semester Regular/Supplementary Examinations, October/November - 2017

Operating Systems

(Common to Computer Science and Engineering and Information Technology)

Time: 3 hours **Max. Marks: 70**

Note: 1. Question Paper Consists of Two Parts **(Part-A and Part-B)**

2. Answering the Question in **Part-A** is compulsory

3. Answer Any **THREE** Questions From **Part-B**

******

Part A

1. a) Define Operating System. List out the objectives of an operating system. [3M]

b) Describe different attributes of the process. [4M]

c) Define Busy Waiting? How to overcome busy waiting using Semaphore operations. [4M]

d) Write the difference between internal and external fragmentation. [4M]

e) Describe the Safe, unsafe, and deadlock state spaces. [4M]

f) What are the various attributes that are associated with an opened file? [3M]

Part B

2. a) What are the various components of operating system structure and explain the simple and layered approach of operating system in detail. [8M]

b) In a multi programming and time sharing environment, several users share the system simultaneously, This situation can result in various security problem: [8M]

i) What are two such problem?

ii) Can be ensure the same degree of security in a time-shared machine as in a dedicated machine? Justify your answer.

3. a) Name five major activities of an OS with respect to process management and briefly describe why each is required. [8M]

   b) Write in detail about the thread libraries. [8M]

4. a) What is Readers-Writers problem? Give a solution to Readers-Writers problem using Monitors. [8M]

   b) What is a Critical Section problem? Give the conditions that a solution to the critical section problem must satisfy. [8M]

5. a) What is a Virtual Memory? Discuss the benefits of virtual memory technique. [8M]

   b) What is Thrashing? What is the cause of Thrashing? How does the system detect Thrashing? What can the system do to eliminate this problem? [8M]

6. a) What is a deadlock? Consider the deadlock situation that could occur in the dining philosopher's problem when the philosophers obtain the chopsticks one at a time. Discuss how the four necessary conditions for deadlock indeed hold in this setting. What are the solutions for this problem? [8M]

   b) Explain Deadlock Detection scheme for Several Instances of a resource Type. [8M]

7. a) Explain the three allocation methods in file system implementation. Illustrate with proper diagram. [8M]

   b) What are the objectives of file management systems? Explain the file system architecture. [8M]

Code No: RT31055 R13 SET - 2

III B. Tech I Semester Regular/Supplementary Examinations, October/November - 2017

Operating Systems

(Common to Computer Science and Engineering and Information Technology)

Time: 3 hours **Max. Marks: 70**

Note: 1. Question Paper Consists of Two Parts **(Part-A and Part-B)**

2. Answering the Question in **Part-A** is Compulsory

3. Answer Any **THREE** Questions From **Part-B**

******

Part A

1. a) Write various registers used in computer system. [3M]

   b) Identify the situations for preemption of a process. [4M]

   c) What are the functions of mutex semaphore? [3M]

   d) Write the first, best fit memory allocation techniques. [4M]

   e) What are different conditions used in Banker's algorithm. [4M]

   f) Define boot block. How it initiated from disk? [4M]

Part B

2. a) What are the functionalities of operating system? Explain in detail. [8M]

   b) Write about monolithic kernel, layered, and microkernel structures of operating systems and analyze their performance. [8M]

3. a) Perform non preemptive CPU scheduling algorithms on the given snapshot and analyze their performance. [8M]

Process	Arrival Time	Burst Time
1	0	3
2	2	6
3	4	4
4	6	5
5	8	2

b) Write about i) Process Control Block ii) CPU scheduling algorithm evaluation. [8M]

4. a) What is monitor? Explain its functionalities. How it is different from semaphore in implementing synchronization. [8M]

   b) What is Producer Consumer problem? How it can illustrate the classical problem of synchronization? Explain. [8M]

5. a) Explain different structures and page tables with strengths and weaknesses. [8M]

   b) What do you mean by thrashing? Suggest solutions to overcome this in virtual memory. [8M]

6. a) In what way resource allocation graphs are used for detection of deadlocks? Write the algorithm. [8M]

   b) Explain the different techniques to recover the system from deadlock. [8M]

7. a) Write the role of sector sparing in identifying the bad blocks of mass storage. What are the other techniques available for this? [8M]

   b) Discuss in detail the file allocation techniques: sequential, indexed and linked. [8M]

******

Code No: RT31055 R13 SET - 3

III B. Tech I Semester Regular/Supplementary Examinations, October/November - 2017

Operating Systems

(Common to Computer Science and Engineering and Information Technology)

Time: 3 hours **Max. Marks: 70**

Note: 1. Question Paper Consists of Two Parts **(Part-A and Part-B)**

2. Answering the Question in **Part-A** is Compulsory

3. Answer Any **THREE** Questions From **Part-B**

******

Part A

1. a) What are the various security issues that arise in multiprogramming and time shared systems? [3M]

b) Write the benefits of multithreaded programming. [3M]

c) Give the Peterson's solution to the Critical section problem. [4M]

d) Explain why sharing a reentrant module is easier, when segmentation is used than when pure paging is used. [4M]

e) Write about Resource-Allocation graph. [4M]

f) Briefly explain the indexed allocation method. [4M]

Part B

2. a) Differentiate protection and security. [4M]

b) Explain the features of a distributed operating system. [8M]

c) Explain models of distributed systems. [4M]

3. a) Explain the actions taken by a thread library to context-switch between user level threads. [8M]

b) What is a Scheduler? Explain different CPU Schedulers. [8M]

4. a) What is a semaphore? List the types of semaphores and Show that, if the wait() and signal() semaphore operations are not executed atomically, then mutual exclusion may be violated. [8M]

   b) How to implement process synchronization using i)Test and Set ii) SWAP iii) Lock instructions? Explain with Pseudo code. [8M]

5. a) What is paged segmentation? How it can be implemented? Discuss its advantages. [8M]

   b) Write about Least Recently Used page replacement algorithm all its variants with an example. [8M]

6. a) Explain deadlock avoidance process using Resource-Allocation-Graph. [8M]

   b) Explain Deadlock detection algorithm with an example. [8M]

7. a) How to organize the mass storage? Explain [8M]

Code No: RT31055 R13 SET - 4

III B. Tech I Semester Regular/Supplementary Examinations, October/November - 2017

Operating Systems

(Common to Computer Science and Engineering and Information Technology)

Time: 3 hours **Max. Marks: 70**

Note: 1. Question Paper Consists of Two Parts **(Part-A and Part-B)**

2. Answering the Question in **Part-A** is Compulsory

3. Answer Any **THREE** Questions From **Part-B**

******

Part A

1. a) What is the importance of Real-Time Embedded systems? [3M]

b) Define Cooperating process? What is the environment need in Cooperating processes? [4M]

c) What are the three requirements that a solution to the critical section problem must satisfy? [3M]

d) What is the purpose of Paging and Page tables? [4M]

e) Discuss the usage of wait-for graph method. [4M]

f) Explain the bit vector representation of free space management. [4M]

Part B

2. a) Explain the various types of system calls provided by an operating system. [8M]

b) Explain the Dual-Mode operation of an operating system. [8M]

3. a) Explain in detail Inter Process Communication models. [3M]

b) Explain the Round Robin scheduling algorithm with a suitable example. [8M]

4. a) By illustrating the structure of process P1, explain the Petersons solution to critical section problem. [8M]

b) State the Critical Section problem. Illustrate the software based solution to the Critical Section problem. [8M]

5. a) Consider the following page reference string:

   1,2,3,4,2,1,5,6,2,1,2,3,7,6,3,2,1,2,3,6

   How many page faults would occur for the optimal page replacement algorithm, assuming three frames and all frames are initially empty. [8M]

   b) Discuss various issues related to the allocation of frames to processes. [8M]

6. a) Explain deadlock avoidance using banker's algorithm with suitable example. [8M]

   b) How to Recover From Deadlock situations? Discuss in detail. [8M]

7. a) Explain various file access methods with suitable examples. [8M]

   b) Discuss various issues involved in selecting appropriate disk scheduling algorithm. [8M]

*****

Code No: RT31055 R13 SET - 1

III B. Tech I Semester Supplementary Examinations, October/November- 2018

Operating Systems

(Common to Computer Science Engineering and Information Technology)

Time: 3 hours **Max. Marks: 70**

Note: 1. Question Paper Consists of Two Parts **(Part-A and Part-B)**

2. Answering the Question in **Part-A** is Compulsory

3. Answer Any **THREE** Questions From **Part-B**

******

Part A

1. a) Mention the objectives and functions of an operating system. [3M]

b) Define preemption and non-preemption. [4M]

c) What is Semaphore? Mention its properties. [4M]

d) List the steps needed for page replacement. [4M]

e) What is deadlock? What are the schemes used in operating system to handle deadlocks? [3M]

f) What are the various file accessing methods? [4M]

Part B

2. a) Explain the operating system structure and its functions. [8M]

b) Briefly Explain the different types of systems: parallel systems, distributed systems and real-time systems? [8M]

3. a) Explain the steps involved in process creation and process termination. [8M]

b) Demonstrate FIFO and Round Robin CPU scheduling algorithms with suitable example. [8M]

4. a) What is the critical section? What are the minimum requirements that should be satisfied by a solution to critical section problem? [8M]

b) Give a solution for readers-writers problem using conditional critical regions? [8M]

5. a) Explain the concept of demand paging in detail with neat diagrams. [8M]

b) Given memory partition of 100 KB, 500 KB, 200 KB and 600 KB (in order). [8M]

Show with neat sketch how would each of the first-fit, best-fit and worst fit algorithms place processes of 412 KB, 317 KB, 112 KB and 326 KB (in order).

6. a) Explain the techniques used to prevent the deadlocks. [8M]

b) Explain Banker's deadlock-avoidance algorithm with an illustration. [8M]

7. a) Discuss the different file allocation methods with suitable example. [8M]

b) Compare and contrast free space management and swap space management. [8M]

*****